Modern Feminist Theory: an Introduction

Modern Feminist Theory

An Introduction

Jennifer Rich

$\mathcal{HEB}$ ☼ **Humanities-Ebooks**

First published by *Humanities-Ebooks, LLP,*
Tirril Hall, Tirril, Penrith CA10 2JE

2nd edn, revised, 2014

The Pdf Ebook is available to private purchasers from http://www.humanities-ebooks.co.uk and to libraries from Ebrary, EBSCO and MyiLibrary.com.

ISBN 978-1-84760-023-3 Pdf Ebook
ISBN 978-1-84760-126-1 Kindle Ebook
ISBN 978-1-84760-308-1 ePub Ebook
ISBN 978-1-84760-341-8 Paperback

Contents

Introduction

At a cocktail party, a discussion of the definition of feminism was raging without a clear conclusion. Some participants suggested that feminism was the demand for 'equal rights'; some that it involved the dismantling of the 'sex/gender' system; still others that it was the unending struggle against male domination in all its forms. Finally, an eight-year-old who had been listening intently to the conversation disingenuously asked the following—'isn't feminism the belief that women are human beings'? At this question, all conversation stopped; the eight-year-old *boy* had hit the nail on the head. All that was needed was a slight emendation of his interrogative—that is that feminism IS the radical belief that women are human beings.

While this definition might seem painfully obvious, it nevertheless touches on the trajectory of feminist theory of the last forty years, what we will call 'second-wave feminism'. All feminist theory has been concerned in divergent ways and through divergent means with establishing the 'subject-position' of women. To say that a woman is a human being is to disentangle her from the dangerous nexus of objectification, prejudice and cultural norms and it is, most importantly, to establish her on an equal footing with 'men' and all that this subject-position provides. The rehumanization of 'woman' is the goal of the feminist theoreticians that we will consider in this volume.

Initial Articulations of the 'Woman' Problem

Virginia Woolf

Virginia Woolf is perhaps best known as one of the twentieth-century's most important modernist novelists. Until the 1970s, her novels were far more widely read than her feminist essays (and the novels still enjoy much deserved popularity); since the advent of second-wave feminism, however, her feminist works such a *A Room of One's Own* and *Three Guineas*—have been reestablished as central reading for students of feminist theory. For the purposes of our discussion, we will consider *A Room of One's Own,* a text that best articulates the materialist-based analysis of female oppression that will prove one of the most significant influences on feminist methodology of the second wave.

A Room of One's Own

Written in 1928 for a lecture at Girton College, Cambridge, *A Room of One's Own* is Woolf's comprehensive answer to the 'woman problem': the accusation of female inferiority in the arts and elsewhere. Woolf was asked to talk to the female students at Girton College—the only college in the U.K. that in 1928 admitted women—about the issue of 'women and fiction'. In her text, Woolf reconstructs the thinking process that leads to the pronouncement that serves both as the title of her talk and its main argument: in order to write fiction, a woman must have a room of her own and £500 per year. Although seemingly obvious (of course in order to write fiction you need space and money) Woolf's argument necessarily involves disputing age-old observations of women's capabilities and also encompasses a profound materialist analysis of the condition of women's existence—at Girton and elsewhere.

In novelistic fashion, Woolf recreates for her audience the grad-ual step-by-step evolution of her thinking in the course of her text. Although an essay, Woolf departs from linear argumentation: she judges herself incapable of 'fulfill[ing] ... the first duty of a lec-turer—to hand you after an hour's discourse a nugget of pure truth to wrap up between the pages of your notebooks and keep on the man-telpiece forever' (3). The fact that the first word of *A Room of One's Own* is 'but'—an interruptive conjunction that usually indicates a shift in thinking—only prefigures Woolf's refusal to engage in tra-ditional so-called 'rational' discourse. This introductory 'but' is no accident, but rather signals a departure from male-defined thinking practices, ones which proceed from 'a' to 'b' without any residue of the thinking process that underlies such an approach. Woolf's method is consciously messy: she wills the reader to experience with her *her* thinking process, and thus to be able more fully to appreciate the far-reaching implications of her seemingly facile conclusion (about the room and the money):

> I am going to do what I can to show you how I arrived at this opinion about the room and the money. I am going to develop in your presence as fully and freely as I can the train of thought that led me to think this. Perhaps if I lay bare the ideas, the prejudices, that lie behind this statement you fill find that they have some bearing upon women and some upon fiction. At any rate, when a subject is highly controversial—and any question about sex is that—one cannot hope to tell the truth. One can only show how one come to hold whatever opinion one does hold. (4)

As promised, Woolf starts with an account of her visit to 'Oxbridge'—a fictional combination of Oxford and Cambridge She recounts sitting 'at the bank of a river', her head bowed down by the task before her'—that is, coming to a meaningful conclusion about the topic of women and fiction. An idea eventually comes to her, and sends her on an agitated walk towards a library to examine a manuscript. Unfortunately, her idea and her sojourn to the library is interrupted by a beadle—a security officer—who stops Woolf because she has committed the unpardonable sin of walking on the grass rather than the gravel. While seemingly insignificant, the Beadle interrupts her process of thought—it sends, as she says, her little thought into 'hiding'. In this way, the Beadle represents the strictures that prevent women from thinking in significant ways. Just as they can not walk on the grass, they cannot sign their names to their works; they are expected to take care of children, and so on.

This anecdote is just one of the ways that Woolf demonstrates the materialist bases of women's oppression, and most importantly, that this oppression is not a result of the natural order of things, but is the inevitable product of social relationships and access to wealth. The most persuasive example of this material inequity is Woolf's discussion—humorously enough—of the differences between the food served at the Men's college at Oxbridge and the women's college.

While her discussion inspires hunger in the reader and in the writer (filet of soles, partridges, and a wonderful meringue are served) what is also inspires is a sense of 'the good life'—of material comfort and the psychological feelings of confidence and aptitude that come with such comforts:

> And thus by degrees was lit, halfway down the spine, which is the seat of the soul, ... the more profound subtle and subterranean glow, which is the rich yellow flame of rational intercourse. No need to hurry. No need to sparkle. No need to be anybody but oneself. We are all going to heaven and Vandyck[1] is of the company ... (Woolf 11)

Woolf pairs the discussion of dinner at the men's college with supper at the women's college. She includes a similar description of the food served and the differences between the two become depressingly apparent:

> Here was my soup. It was a plain gravy soup. There was nothing to stir the fancy in that. One could have seen through the transparent liquid any pattern that there might have been on

---

1   Anthony Vandyck (1599–1641) was the royal portraitist in seventeenth-century England. He was thus associated with aristocracy, comfort and privilege.

the plate itself. But there was no pattern. The plate was plain.
(Woolf 17)

It soon becomes obvious that unlike the feelings of comfort and
security inspired by the men's college dinner, this supper would in
no way inspire such feelings. Woolf describes the querulous and
'dubious' state of mind that is the inevitable result of dining on
mutton instead of partridge:

> One cannot think well, love well, sleep well, if one has not
> dined well. The lamp in the spine does not light on beef and
> prunes. We are all *probably* going to heaven, and Vandyck is,
> we *hope*, to meet us round the next corner—that is the dubious
> and qualifying state of mind that beef and prunes at the end of
> the day's work breed between them. (Woolf 19)

Woolf's focus on food telescopes the clear material differences
between the men and women's colleges—differences which must
result in significant psychological and social inequities both within
and without the academy. In order to understand fully the character
of women's oppression, however, Woolf explores the history of
women's lives and their relationship to material wealth.

Returning from her visit to Oxbridge, Woolf hastens to the British
Museum; her research question is simple—why are women poor?
Expecting to find a ready and reliable answer at the premier research
library of Europe and Great Britain, Woolf soon discovers that the
available information is paltry and biased. Consulting a famous his-
torian's monumental *History of England*, for example, she notes only
three entries about women—all of which suggest that women were
considered nothing more than chattel:

> I went … to the shelf where the histories were and took down
> one of the latest, Professor Trevelyan's *History of England*.
> Once more I looked up 'Women', found 'position of,' and
> turned to the pages indicated. 'Wife beating,' I read, 'was a
> recognized right of man, and was practiced without shame by
> high as well as low …' (Woolf 44)

Unable to find substantive information that would tell her what women did, in her words, 'between eight in the morning and eight at night', Woolf must invent a historical example to illustrate the disparities in wealth and opportunity. Imagining that Shakespeare had a brilliant sister called Judith, Woolf constructs an elaborate fantasy of what would have happened to her had Judith—like William—desired to write and go into the theatre. This is perhaps one of the most poignant moments in *A Room of One's Own*—for, unlike William, Judith cannot possibly fare well as an aspiring *female* writer in renaissance England:

> Let me imagine since fact are so hard to come by, what would have happened had Shakespeare had a wonderfully gifted sister, called Judith, let us say … She was as adventurous, as imaginative, as agog to see the world as he was. But she was not sent to school…. She picked up a book now and then, one of her brother's perhaps, and read a few pages. But then her parents came in and told her to mend the stockings or mind the stew and not moon about with books and papers. (Woolf 49)

Given this introduction, it is easy to see where this story leads: predictably enough, Judith is engaged to a 'neighbouring son of a wool stapler' against her wishes, runs away, attempts to find work in the theatre, finds herself pregnant instead and, as a result, commits suicide. 'That', as Woolf writes, would be 'more or less … how the story would run … if a woman in Shakespeare's day had had Shakespeare's genius' (50). Woolf points out that such genius is not usually to be found in 'the uneducated working classes': genius is not the miraculous gift of a divine presence but most often develops among the lettered leisure class—those that have rooms of their own, and independent means.

Woolf's argument leaves women of her day at a significant aesthetic disadvantage: few in 1928 would have been in the economic position that Woolf stipulates is necessary for artistic creation. And if we are to take Woolf at her word, then how do we make sense of Charlotte Bronte, or Jane Austen, for example, especially since both were not blessed with either independent means or rooms? Her answer is somewhat equivocal: she acknowledges that occasionally—

for inexplicable reasons—an 'Emily Bronte or Robert Burns[1] blazes out and proves its [genius's] presence' in the lower classes (51), but that this is very much the exception rather than the rule. Also, when women such as Charlotte Bronte write in conditions of extremity, their writing shows the symptoms of its context: it is angry, bitter, and because of this, ultimately, a failure.

For Woolf, the successful writer is one that overcomes the restrictions or his or her gender—who is, in his or her mind, androgynous. Woolf introduces this idea through describing a banal everyday occurrence—a man and woman getting into a taxi. Seeing the two genders united, even in an event of incredible ordinariness, 'eases the mind'; it provides a welcome relief from 'thinking of one sex as distinct from the other' (100). Such mental segregation leads not to the poetry of Shakespeare, but to the distorted sputterings of a mad Bertha[2]. But, this androgyny is only possible when both sexes are given the opportunities for self-realization; one cannot think androgynously on a dinner of mutton and prunes, for example. So, for Woolf, a heavy task lies before us; Shakespeare's sister will not come—such genius is not possible—within a social system in which women are admonished not to think or create. To make a Judith Shakespeare emerge, we must have the 'courage to write exactly what we think' and in this way encourage a 'habit of freedom'—a frame of mind freed from the demands of gender and open to the possibilities of a transcendent humanness. *A Room of One's Own* is a call to arms (or rooms) for the female students addressed in this essay; it is also, however, an indictment of the mental and material circumstances in women's lives that prevent the expression of their aesthetic creativity.

1   Emily Bronte (1818–1848) and Robert Burns (1759–1796) were writers of considerable fame who were born into unpropitious circumstances: Burns came from a poor Scottish family and Bronte from a middle-class, conservative English family. Emily Bronte is most famously the author of *Wuthering Heights* (1847) and Robert Burns was a working-class Scotsman who wrote poetry in the early 18th century.
2   Bertha is a character in Charlotte Bronte's *Jane Eyre*; Woolf pinpoints her as a prime example of how anger can distort the creative process: she is a mad wife locked in an attic, and as such, for Woolf, seems to be Bronte's alter-ego, see pages 74–78 in *A Room of One's Own*.

Simone de Beauvoir

Although the author of one of the most important feminist texts in the 20th century, *The Second Sex,* Simone de Beauvoir did not consider herself a 'feminist'. In an interview Beauvoir remarks that after writing *The Second Sex* in 1949,

> I said that I was not a feminist because I believed that the problems of women would resolve themselves automatically in the context of socialist development. By feminist I meant fighting on specifically feminine issues independently of the class struggle. I still hold the same view today. In my defini-tion, feminists are women—or even men, too—who are fight-ing to change women's condition in association with the class struggle but independently as well. (Moi 92)

In 1949, Beauvoir was intimately involved in both the struggle for socialism and also existentialism—a philosophy that advocates the radical subjectivity of the individual. *The Second Sex* is more obviously an integration of existentialist issues (subjectivity vs. objectivity) within a historical framework that specifically concerns the situation of women. It is an exhaustive discussion that ranges from an analysis of the biology of woman to her social status. Its introduction, however, provides a brief yet profound analysis of the governing assumption implied by its title—precisely that the situation of 'woman' was a by-product of the dualist thinking characteristic of Western (male-dominated) philosophy of the last 5000 years.

Introduction to The Second Sex

One of the most famous statements to issue from Beauvoir's *Second Sex* is her pithy claim that 'one is not born a woman; one becomes one' (*The Second Sex* 243). The introduction to *The Second Sex* provides the philosophical rationale for this statement. As Beauvoir asserts, she is not seeking a definition of the feminine; in fact, she could not care less about the so-called problem of women. Instead, she wishes to understand how woman became a problem, and more specifically, what is connoted by the notion of woman as a category of species and thought:

> For a long time I have hesitated to write a book on woman. The subject is irritating, especially to women; and it is not new. Enough ink has been spilled in the quarrelling over feminism, now practically over, and perhaps we should say no more about it. (1)

Early in the introduction, Beauvoir retraces the definitions of woman; she notes quite surprisingly that woman, for example, has been defined primarily through her physicality (*tota mulier in utero*). Also, she alludes to Platonic thought in noting that woman, and by extension, femininity has been considered an 'essence' that is threatened in varying degrees by social change and by feminism. This search for a definition of woman leads Beauvoir eventually to posit that woman cannot be defined in and of herself. Her definition rests on woman's particular situatedness—that of being '*other*' to man. For Beauvoir, a woman can only be a woman (in the conventional sense) when she is differentiated from man:

> A man is in the right in being a man; it is the woman who is in the wrong. It amounts to this: just as for the ancients there was an absolute vertical to which the oblique was defined, so there is an absolute human type, the masculine. (13)

The wrongness of woman—the fact that she is the oblique to the male vertical—lies in her physicality. While man can transcend the physical, woman is trapped within it: 'Woman has ovaries, a uterus: these peculiarities imprison her in her subjectivity, circumscribe her within the limits of her own nature. It is often said that she thinks with her glands' (13). Not only is woman limited to the 'peculiarities' of her own nature, but this nature is generalized into a category that is anti-intellectual at its core. In this way, it replicates the age-old mind/body division that originated in Ancient Greek philosophy, particularly with Plato. While men were able to transcend the physical, women were not thought capable of doing so; hence, the physical—and its most potent manifestation in the sex act—became intimately associated with the ontology (the being) of woman. Beauvoir notes this in her remark that 'for him [man] she [woman] is sex—absolute sex, no less' (13).

This assignment of women to 'sex' carries within it a broader ontological categorization, one that allows man to occupy the subject position by virtue of his association with the mind, while woman rests within the category of 'other' imprisoned by her physicality. As Beauvoir notes: 'He is the subject, he is the Absolute—she is the Other' (13).

Beauvoir is careful to note that the notion of 'Other' is not limited to the situation of women. It characterizes the dualistic nature of Western thought. Alluding to Georg Frederic Hegel, a nineteenth-century German philosopher, for example, Beauvoir remarks that 'we find in consciousness itself a fundamental hostility toward every other consciousness; the subject can be posed only in being opposed—he sets himself up as the essential, as opposed to the other, the inessential, the object' (14). Thus, minorities—Jews and people of colour, for example—are understood as 'other' in a racist epistemology that posits Christian whiteness as the norm. The concept of the other is universally present simply because a subject position is predicated upon objectification: one can only be a 'subject' if there is an 'other' against which the subject can define itself. This ontological dependence is perhaps more understandable if we remember the master-slave dialectic posited by Hegel. As Hegel noted, a master can only be a master in relationship to a slave—and vice versa. Thus, this identity is dialectical—drawing its definition from a relationship of reciprocity.

It is precisely this relationship of reciprocity that prevents women from wanting to leave their status as *other*. Just as a slave draws some benefits from his relationship to the master—as meagre as these may be—so do women. Part of this acceptance of otherness also derives from the absence of a female community; women, unlike other subjected groups, do not have a sense of their history and unity. For women, there is no 'we'. Women have always been subjected to men, but they also have always been in a relationship of dependence and filiation to men. Men constitute their families: they are their fathers, their husbands and their sons. As such, women cannot imagine an identity independent of men:

> They [women] have no past, no history, no religion of their own ... [t]hey live dispersed among the males, attached through residence, housework, economic condition and social standing to certain men—fathers and husbands—more firmly than they are to other women. (15)

Not only are women linked to men through family but also through economic and social dependence. As Beauvoir notes, their status is defined by and through males. They are thus 'quite pleased' with their role as other because it gives them benefits which are unattainable except through this role. Yet, as Beauvoir notes, women's evolution toward subjectivity is necessary to escape the subjections of 'otherness' and more importantly, to gain 'full membership in the human race'. For Beauvoir, reaching subjectivity means becoming a human being; in this conception, Beauvoir links her feminist analysis philosophically to existentialism—especially its notion of a radically subjective individuality. Beauvoir's conclusion also nicely links to the conversation alluded to in the introduction to this volume. Had she been a part of the aforementioned debate around feminism, she no doubt would have agreed with the eight-year old's definition—that it is that feminism must be the understanding of women as human beings (and not objects).

Radical Feminism

Radical feminism arose out of the consciousness-raising movements of the 1960s, where women, for the first time, theorized their 'second-class' status within the male-dominated social world (the patriarchy). Radical feminism attempted to combat patriarchal (male/anti-woman) dominance in all of its manifestations—both in the realm of politics and in personal experience. The mantra 'the personal is political' became a rallying cry for radical feminists who saw evidence of male domination in the home as well as the larger social world. Even as mundane a task as dishwashing can have a political overtone when looked at through a radically feminist lens. Consider this question: If dishwashing is without question considered a woman's role in the home, what does this say about the power dynamics operating between men and women both in the home and in the wider world in general—the personal is political!

Kate Millett, *Sexual Politics*

Kate Millett's *Sexual Politics* was a ground breaking and comprehensive analysis of the representation and practice of male domination. Written in the 1970s, it focused on the representation of women in literature, as well as providing an extensive theory and history of sexual politics and the sexual revolution. *Sexual Politics* now is most influential for its literary analysis. It is the primary forerunner for feminist literary criticism—analyses that pay careful attention to the power dynamics underlying the representation of men and women in literature.

Millett's first chapter is a critique of those she considers the most macho and misogynistic writers of the twentieth century—Henry

Miller, D. H. Lawrence and Norman Mailer.[1] Many of the passages that Millett chooses to read closely are graphic erotica from these various writers. For this reason, I will not reproduce any of them here. What Millett reveals in her reading of these passages, however, is the denigration of the female that fuels the erotic in these works. Women in these passages are rarely referred to by name but reduced either to animals—'she was hungry, like a lean rat' or parts of the body 'I took her mouth at last' (11). Also, the heroic men who engage in these acts of copulation are not strengthened by them, but weakened. In Norman Mailer's *American Dream,* for example, Rojack (the hero) is strengthened only through the murder of his maid/lover, Ruta:

> Once almost a 'loser', he is rejuvenated and remade through the act of murder: he wins a fight with a black gangster who cowers before him, a fortune at the tables at Las Vegas, and the love of a nightclub singer who wants him to make her a lady. … In fact, Mailer's *An American Dream* is an exercise in how to kill your wife and be happy ever after. (15)

Through discussing Mailer's and other writers' definition of the female, Millett provides a definition of what it is to be male—at least in the eyes of the writers that she considers. Maleness consists in being 'master, hero, brute and pimp' (17). Real men do not cherish women, but rather use them to satisfy their physical longings. Men and women in this view are in a relationship of 'feudal servitude'.

Apart from her lengthy discussion of literary representations of women, Millett's text also contains an ambitious chapter that attempts to provide an overarching theory of patriarchal society 'where male shall dominate female, and elder male shall dominate younger' (25). Millett sees this dynamic as underwriting and operating as an 'institution', one which is 'so deeply entrenched as to run through all other political, social or economic forms, whether of caste or class, feudality or bureaucracy, just as it pervades all major religions…' (25). Millett

---

1   Few literary critics would equate Lawrence with Miller or Mailer. Millett does so because she chooses to assume that the blind drives of some of Lawrence's characters (usually expressed in what is called 'free indirect discourse') encode the author's values and are endorsed by his novels.

traces patriarchy's workings in the sociological, biological and anthropological realms. In this discussion she focuses on the family as the central factor in the perpetuation of the patriarchy; as she writes,

> Patriarchy's chief institution is the family. It is both a mirror of and a connection with a larger society; a patriarchal unity within a patriarchal whole. Mediating between the individual and social structure, the family effects control and conformity where political and other authorities are insufficient. (33)

The education that both sexes receive in the family *vis a vis* their relationship to one another are simply re-inscribed in the state (via education) and in culture (via ritual). The family is the cornerstone for the pervasive naturalization of this asymmetry of power between male and female.

Millett's arguments influenced radical feminists working in the 1970s in political and social theory as well as feminist literary theory that developed in the late 1970s.

Shulamith Firestone

Shulamith Firestone was another key member of the radical feminist movement of the 1970s and 1980s. Firestone was a founding member of several radical feminist groups, including the New York Radical Feminists and Redstockings in the late 1960s. Firestone's devotion to feminism, like many other feminists, arose out of her participation in the African-American civil rights movement. Her involvement in the fight against Jim Crowism[1] sparked a critical realization of the similarly oppressive structures operating against women. Also, Firestone was struck by the hypocrisy of some civil rights leaders who tended to treat women as second-class citizens in their organizations. For Firestone, the fight for equality must not only include African-American men, but also women as well.

---

1   Jim Crowism was the system of de-facto segregation that operated in the Southern United States after the Civil War and Reconstruction.

The Dialectic of Sex

Written in 1970, *The Dialectic of Sex* is Firestone's attempt to anatomize the roots of female oppression. Its theoretical basis owes much to Marxist theory; in this text, Firestone uses Marx and Engels' theory of class oppression as a medium for the analysis of sexual oppression:

> I have attempted to take the class analysis one step further to its roots in the biological division of the sexes.... As a first step in this direction ... we shall expand Engels' definition of historical materialism .... 'Historical materialism is that view of the course of history which seeks the ultimate cause and the great moving power of all historical events in the dialectic of sex: the division of society into two distinct biological classes for procreative reproduction, and the struggles of these classes with one another' (*The Second Wave* 25)

Although Frederick Engels did consider family dynamics in understanding class structure and consciousness, Firestone centralizes the dialectic of sex—the power relations of the sexes—in the definition of historical materialism[1]. Instead of seeing economic relationships as the basis of human society, as traditional historical materialism does, Firestone insists that the division of the sexes—and the power relations that emanate from this division—are the moving factor of social life. For Firestone, women themselves occupy a class—a sex class—that has been at the mercy of men for centuries:

> The biological family is an inherently unequal power distribution. The need for power leading to the development of classes arises from the psychosexual formation of each individual according to this basic imbalance (*The Second Wave* 23)

---

1   Historical materialism is a philosophy of history that views economic forces as the base upon which all other social structures and relationships are built, such as the family, moral codes, social hierarchies, education, and so on. These social structures and relationships are commonly called the 'superstructure' resting upon the 'base' of economic relationships.

Firestone locates the biological family as the cornerstone of women's oppression. Using Beauvoir's notion of the 'other' (see above), she postulates that females occupy this space because of the 'tyranny of reproduction'—and the division of labour that underwrites this relationship. This subservient status is a result of male control of reproduction. Feminist revolution, for Firestone, must consist of nothing less than the complete reversal of the sex class system. This means that the hegemonic or dominant system of social ordering between the sexes—the patriarchy—must be dismantled:

> Just as to assure the elimination of economic classes requires the revolt of the underclass (the proletariat) ... so to assure the elimination of sexual classes requires the revolt of the underclass (women) and the seizure of control of *reproduction* ... (*The Second Wave* 24)

For Firestone, the seizure of the control of reproduction entailed some radical proposals: one of which was the 'control of the social institutions of childrearing and childbearing'. In practice, this meant the abandonment of traditional marriage in favour of women's collectives that would raise children collectively without male interference (except for the necessary biological contribution for pregnancy to occur). Many radical feminists rejected this separatist mentality in favour of a systematic interrogation of patriarchy from within the existing social structure. Firestone's separatist instincts, among other reasons, led her eventually to cut all ties with radical feminist groups.

Unfortunately, after the *Dialectic of Sex*, Firestone began to suffer from mental illness and ceased to be actively involved in any radical feminist groups. *The Dialectic of Sex*, however, remained widely influential and inspired groups such as RadicalLesbians and the intellectual movement of gynocentrism considered below.

Radicalesbians

Radicalesbians was a group founded in 1970 as a response to Betty Freidan's comments that lesbians constituted a 'lavender menace' to the nascent feminist movement. They initially called themselves 'lavender menace' as a protest against Friedan's remarks and as a way of shocking the feminist movement into an acknowledgement of the lesbian presence within the movement. Even though mainstream feminism during the 1970s and 1980s posed a devastating and far-reaching critique of patriarchal norms, it still retained within it homophobic attitudes that profoundly alienated gay women from full participation in feminism. In part, this was a symptom of a much deeper problem within second-wave feminism: the failure to acknowledge differences among women. The black feminist movement considered below, for example, emerged from the frustration of exclusion that black women felt by 'white' mainstream feminism. Similarly, lesbians felt that their particular experiences were marginalized by feminism's focus on the heterosexual/patriarchal world.

The Woman-Identified Woman

'The Woman-Identified Woman' was a manifesto written for the second Congress to Unite Women held in 1970. Although not invited to participate, the Lavender Menace distributed copies of this manifesto to every audience member and then hijacked the conference proceedings by dousing the lights and taking over the stage. Once the lights came back on, the Lavender Menace formed a line of women with t-shirts stencilled with the name of the group on them. Instead of objecting to this dramatic turn of events, one of the conference's chairwomen, Kate Millett (see above), welcomed this interruption and the conference attendees proceeded to discuss the issues of lesbianism and homophobia for the next two hours.

In this work, Radicalesbians enlarge the definition of lesbian beyond that of a sexual predilection and identity. Asking rhetorically 'what is a lesbian,' they answer that 'a lesbian is the rage of all women condensed to the point of explosion' (*The Second Wave* 153). Generalizing in this way, lesbianism becomes a way of symbolizing every woman's rage and also every woman's route towards independence. Since, according to Radicalesbians, traditional heterosexual norms demand women's subservience to men, lesbianism becomes the label that is attached to women:

> Lesbian is the word, the label, the condition that holds women
> in line. When a woman hears this word tossed her way, she
> knows she is stepping out of line. She knows that she has
> crossed the terrible boundary of her sex role. She recoils, she
> protests, she reshapes her activities to gain approval. Lesbian
> is a label invented by the Man to throw at any woman who
> desires to be his equal, who dares to challenge his preroga-
> tives…who dares to assert the primacy of her own needs. (*The
> Second Wave* 154)

Radicalesbians claim that the division of sexuality into heterosexual
and homosexual domains is a means of control. For a woman,
'lesbian' is a feared label since it carries within it an indictment of
femininity. The lesbian label thus becomes the whipping post to
which any independent woman is tied as punishment for her stepping
out of a traditional female role.

The manifesto calls on women 'to disengage from male-defined
response patterns'. This work must be internal at first: 'In the pri-
vacy of our own psyches, we must cut those cords to the core.' Even
the lesbian—self-identified as such—must transcend the categories
of sexuality provided since 'being a woman' and 'being independent'
are necessarily mutually incompatible. The final passages of 'The
Woman-Identified Woman' implicitly endorse separatism since the
pursuit of identity (as well as happiness) is dependent upon a radical
rejection of patriarchal categorizations not only of sexuality, but also
of gender. This can only happen apart from men because such a rejection demands a new kind of 'room of one's own'—a space in which
women can think as women, and as such, escape what Monique
Wittig calls 'the straight mind'.

Mary Daly

Mary Daly is perhaps one of the most influential voices in radical
feminism. She is the author of several ground breaking—and
consciousness-altering books; among them are *Pure Lust, Beyond God*

the Father, and the text that we will consider below—*Gyn/Ecology: The Metaethics of Radical Feminism* (1975). Daly's background would seem hardly to qualify her as a radical feminist. She received doctorates in philosophy and theology from the University of Fribourg, Switzerland, and then held a position at Boston College, a conservative Catholic college. She received tenure at Boston College, but was later denied promotion beyond the associate professor level—most likely due to her radical writings, especially her book *Gyn/Ecology*. Also, she consistently refused to allow male students to attend her classes at Boston College, claiming that their presence dampened discussion about feminist issues. She was finally sued for this practice and resigned from Boston College in 1999.

Gyn/Ecology

While Daly's scholarship is lambasted as irresponsible and hopelessly biased, she nevertheless laid the groundwork for a uniquely radical feminist ethics—one that rejects wholeheartedly the patriarchal myths that structure the social world.[1] As her title suggests, her intent in Gyn/Ecology is to unearth the lost female ethics—what Daly might call the voice and rage of the Crone or Hag--words she rescues from their negative, patriarchally-inspired connotations. As she writes in her new 1999 introduction to *Gyn/Ecology:*

> *Gyn/Ecology* can be Seen/Heard as a Thunderbolt of Rage that I hurled into the world against the patriarchs who have never ceased to massacre women and our Sister the Earth. I wrote it in a Time of Great Rage, when women were Wildly Moving, Sinspired by their Creative Fury. (Daly xxxi)

As the above passage makes clear, part of Daly's critique of the patriarchy takes as its form the creation of neologisms—such as 'Sinspired'. According to Daly, such neologisms were formed as a natural process of breaking with patriarchal systems of thought. The commonplace words of patriarchal culture and their agreed-upon

---

1   For an important and interesting critique of Daly's Eurocentric approach to women's history, see the February 2000 issue of the journal, *Off Our Backs*.

definitions could not begin to convey the changes in thinking that Daly was both experiencing and communicating in writing *Gyn/Ecology*. Her neologisms and wordplay, she writes, 'seem to have a life of their own. They seem to want to break the bonds of conventional usage, to break the silence imposed upon their own Backgrounds. They become palpable, powerful and it seems that they are tired of allowing me to "use" them and cry out for a role reversal' (Daly xix).

Hagography

The creation of new words or the redefinition of old ones is simply a manifestation of Daly's much broader and more ambitious plan—to 'exorcise' the patriarchal control of meaning—especially in reference to women's experience. Thus, Daly reclaims words that have a particularly negative connotation in the traditional social world, and uses them as powerful weapons against patriarchal thinking. Much of this takes the form of researching the original meanings of words such as 'haggard', 'crone', 'hag', 'glamour', and finding within their etymology a powerful source for a uniquely feminist outlook. Thus, for example, Daly's investigation of the word 'haggard' results in the discovery that the original definition denoted an 'intractable person, especially: a woman reluctant to yield to wooing' (Daly 15).

Although such etymological rediscovery might seem insignificant, it is an integral part of Daly's exorcism—for how can anyone escape the mental fetters of thousands of years of conventional thinking and meaning without seeking a new language? To use old language is automatically to fall into the trap of old thinking. In order to escape old patterns of patriarchally-inflected thought, Daly not only instanti-ates a new vocabulary, but with it a new epistemology—a new way of thinking about women's experience both in the past and in the present. She names her meta-ethics a hagography, punning on the word 'hagiography'—which refers to the history of the Christian saints. Her hagography reclaims and celebrates those women who have been persecuted for their inassimilability and for their haggard-ness. For Daly, these women are our heroes:

> [h]aggard writing is by and for haggard women, those who are intractable, willful (sic), wanton, unchaste, and, especially, those who are reluctant to yield to wooing. It belongs to the tradition of those who refused to assume the woes of wooed women, who cast off these woes as unworthy of Hags, of Harpies. Haggard women are not man-wooed. As Furies, women in the tradition of Great Hags, reject the curse of compromise. (Daly 16–17)

Hagography not only requires that the feminist scholar revise traditional histories of women and recognize patriarchy's consistent silencing and destruction of the female voice,[1] it also demands a recognition of the processes involved in the construction of founding cultural myths. Daly calls these founding myths 'processions'— the unnatural stabilization of processes of cultural myth-making for purposes of domination through the simple process of repetition and celebration.[2]

One such founding myth that Daly confronts is the Virgin birth in Christianity. Daly traces the origin of this myth to attempts to minimize women's creative capacity in origin stories; the virgin birth strips Mary, in particular, of any creative agency and instead renders her as a passive receptacle for an exclusively male version of parthenogenesis. Mary's story is only an extreme manifestation of a more general trend in patriarchally-controlled myth-making: the rape of the Goddess.

> The rape of the Goddess in all of her aspects is an almost universal theme in patriarchal myth. Zeus, for example, was a

---

1   Mary Daly has not been innocent of a certain amount of historical irresponsibility, however. Her strong implication that nine million women were burned at the stake during what she calls the 'burning times' is grossly exaggerated (Daly 182).

2   Daly's focus on 'processions' as a description of historical stabilization of cultural processes is indebted to Virginia Woolf's analysis in *Three Guineas*. Woolf famously notes that the 'processions of the sons of educated men, ascending those pulpits, mounting those steps, passing in and out of those doors, preaching, teaching administering justice, practicing medicine, making money' are collectively the engine of the patriarchal social world.

> habitual rapist.... The early patriarchal rapes of the Goddess, in her various manifestations, symbolized the vanquishing of woman-identified society. In the early mythic rapes, the god often assumed a variety of animal forms; the sense of violence/ violation is almost tangible. In christianity [sic], this theme is refined—disguised almost beyond recognition. (Daly 85)

For Daly, Mary is a non-entity in the Christian creation story. She, like other 'goddesses' referred to above, has had her creative powers stripped away. So passive is Mary that she is not even raped physically—her 'violation' occurs psychologically. As Daly notes,

> In the charming story of the 'Annunciation' the angel Gabriel appears to the terrified young girl, announcing that she has been chosen to become the mother of God (sic). Her response to this sudden proposal from the godfather is totalled non-resistance: 'Let it be done according to thy word.' Physical rape is not necessary when the mind/will/spirit has already been invaded. (85)

Mary is not only agency-less, but is also perpetually indebted since she has been wiped clean of 'original sin' in order to be a fit receptacle for the birth of Christ. Thus, the goddess is no longer the independent creator of divine life, but rather a handmaiden to a power always greater than her own.

Daly does not confine her analysis to Western myths in *Gyn/ Ecology* but also explores the effects of patriarchal cultural norms and myths on women in non-Western cultures. She pays particular attention to 'gyn-atrocities' such as the Indian practice of Suttee[1] and African female genital mutilation. Her discussion of Suttee focuses not so much on the cultural origins of this practice, but rather the way in which Western anthropologists and historians have interpreted suttee. In many of these interpretations—written by both men and women—Daly detects a disconcerting sympathy with the oppressor and a concomitant valorisation of female sacrifice. In suttee Daly dis-

---

1   Suttee was legally banned in 1829 and is rarely practiced today. It was a Hindu practice wherein widows were expected to immolate themselves on their husband's funeral pyre.

cerns a violent contempt for independent women in this practice, a contempt that she argues is not unique to Indian culture. The fact that Western scholar treat this practice with such respect is testimony to a shared denigration of female independence. Daly uses the following quotation of a 1960 discussion of suttee as a telling example of unthinking Western tolerance and even celebration of this practice:

> In many, many cases, the widow walked into the fire *proudly* and by *deliberate choice.* This was her way of showing the depth of her *affection,* her *devotion,* her *fidelity.* It was a strange way, and to us a gravely *mistaken* one. But leaving aside the *inappropriateness* of the action and looking at the motive, dare we say that these women of the East knew less of *true love* than their Western sisters. [Daly's emphasis] (124)

The words that Daly chooses to emphasize here are those that seem to celebrate the widow's presumed 'choice' in committing suicide. The authors of this passage also position the widow's sacrifice as an act of love, thus minimizing the compulsory nature of this act. According to Daly, widowhood was not a real choice for Indian women: widows were routinely vilified for simply surviving their husbands.

Daly's analysis of Indian suttee, like her later analyses of the medieval European witch-craze and African genital mutilation, relies on a presumption of intentionality on the part of men perpetuating these practices. All of these cultural practices are boiled down to a conspiratorial metanarrative (grand story)—that of men (the patriarchy) at all points in history and at all cultural contexts doing all they can to overthrow or minimize women's independent power. This kind of conspiratorial lens does not allow for a full understanding of the network of practices and/or beliefs in which a cultural practice of any kind is imbedded. It is impossible to understand a cultural practice outside of its local determinants, and this is exactly what Daly attempts to do in her analyses of suttee, genital mutilation, and other practices. Also, her 'meta-ethics' suffers from being defined through negation: whatever is associated with the patriarchy is necessarily bad and therefore, whatever condemns the patriarchy and privileges the female is necessarily good. This is simply an inversion of the male-female dichotomy that Beauvoir points to in *The Second Sex*. Rather than the female being the negative term in this binary, the male is now the negative. But the binary here still remains intact, and as such, an epistemology of binarisms/duality is not challenged.

Black Feminism

One issue that troubled the mainstream feminism in the 1970s was its minimization of the unique experience of black women. White women were, for the most part, fighting on the front of sexual discrimination. Black women, in contrast, were fighting on several different fronts—those of race, sex and class. While white feminists were for the most part solidly middle-class, black feminists usually came from working-class backgrounds. Thus, in many ways, the concerns of white feminists were at odds with the issues facing black feminists. And while white feminists extolled the mantra that 'we are all women', black feminists saw this universalisation as a convenient way of marginalizing and ignoring their particular concerns and issues.

One of the clearest articulations of the concerns of black women was a manifesto written by the 'Combahee River Collective', a group formed in 1974 and named after a slave revolt led by Harriet Tubman[1] in 1863. Poignantly, the central issue that motivated the collective's politics was the rehumanisation of black women; as they write,

> Above all else, our politics initially sprang from the shared belief that Black women are inherently valuable, and that our liberation is a necessity not as an adjunct to somebody else's but because of our need as human persons for autonomy. This may seem so obvious as to sound simplistic, but it is apparent that no other ostensibly progressive movement has ever considered our specific oppression as a priority or worked seri-

---

1   Harriet Tubman is known as the mother of the 'underground railroad'—a system that aided the escape of southern slaves to the Northern states. Harriet Tubman—herself a former slave—led more than one thousand African-American slaves to freedom.

ously for the ending of that oppression. (*This Bridge Called My Back: Writings by Radical Women of Color [BCMB]* 212)

As this statement notes, it is not only white women who have ignored the particular historical conditions of oppression for black women. Black feminism originally issued from the civil rights movement for many of the same reasons that mainstream 'white' feminism did: the denigration of female participants in the movement as second-class citizens. Unlike white feminists, however, black feminists could not find a haven for their concerns within mainstream feminism for the reasons articulated above. The Combahee River Collective makes clear that for feminism to be palatable to black women, it must recognize the multiple fronts of oppression that black women daily experience. Black women, unlike white women, must not only fight white men, but also black men, white women, racism, classism, and in some cases, homophobia:

> We exist as women who are Black who are feminists, each stranded for the moment, working independently because there is not yet an environment in the society remotely congenial to our struggle—because, being on the bottom, we would have to do what no one else has done: we would have to fight the world. (Wallace qtd. in *BCMB*, 215)

The first step in this mammoth struggle is simply to recognize the specificity of black women's experiences. To pay attention to black women—to take their concerns seriously—was (and perhaps still is) a revolutionary act; as the manifesto explains, 'to be recognized as human, levelly human, is enough' (*BCMB* 212). Such recognition insists on 'making visible' the 'multilayered texture of Black women's lives' (*BMCB* 212). In particular, it insists on examining those habits of thought that objectify black women, both in mainstream feminism and in the wider culture in general. The Combahee River Collective takes careful aim at the multiple sites of oppression that black women experience—first and foremost, they challenge the 'white women's movement' to address its own 'superficial comprehension' of the issues facing black women. The Collective does not, however, ignore the sexism within the black community itself, and, as difficult as it is, it demands that black males be held accountable for their denigration of black women. In sum, the Collective's statement is a call-to-attention for white and black women—one that significantly altered the critical and social landscape of mainstream feminism for years to come.

Audre Lorde

A brilliant poet, scholar and writer, Audre Lorde was one of the most active thinkers and writers in the early days of black feminism. No doubt inspired by the Combahee River Collective, Lorde's most famous articles draw on personal instances of marginalization and the desire to hold white women accountable for their actions towards black women. In her 'An Open Letter to Mary Daly,' for example, Lorde takes Daly to task for her trivialization of the historical experiences of black women in her book, *Gyn/Ecology* (see above). As Lorde explains,

> To imply … that all women suffer the same oppression simply because we are women, is to lose sight of the many varied tools of patriarchy. It is to ignore how those tools are used by women without awareness against each other … What you excluded from *Gyn/Ecology* dismissed my heritage and the heritage of all other non-european [sic] women, and denied the real connections that exist between all of us. (*BMCB* 95)

Lorde links the 'devaluation' suffered by Daly's omission of any discussion of black female experience and the deities (goddesses) relevant to African culture to the complex ways in which patriarchy in general denies the humanity of black women. This denial, Lorde contends, is literally and figuratively life-threatening: 'When patriarchy dismisses us, it encourages our murderers. When radical lesbian feminist theory dismisses us, it encourages its own demise' (*BCMB* 96).

The Master's Tools Can Never Dismantle the Master's House

Lorde continues her struggle against trivialization in another widely-anthologized article, 'The Master's Tools Can Never Dismantle the Master's House.' In this work, she is again writing in response to an experience of marginalization. She had been asked—at the last minute—to speak at a New York University conference appropriately entitled 'The Second Sex'. Upon arriving at the conference, Lorde found that she was one of two black women assigned to a panel 'The Personal is Political.' Such ghettoization of black women's voices and experience infuriated Lorde and compelled her to ask famously, 'what does it mean when the tools of a racist patriarchy are used to examine the fruits of that same patriarchy? It means that only the most narrow perimeters of change are possible and allowable' (*BCMB* 98). This quasi-rhetorical question leads Lorde to the inevitable answer that is the title of this essay, i.e. the master's tools (the tools of patriarchy—sexism, racism, marginalization) can never dismantle the master's house (the patriarchy).

Because feminists such as Mary Daly and others persist in trivializing black women's experiences, they participate in the systems of oppression against which they are ostensibly fighting. Thus, even as they dismantle one front of oppression, they are at the same time participating in other forms of oppression. Addressing the conference's audience, Lorde asks them to consider what material effect their participation in this conference has had on other women:

> If white American feminist theory need not deal with the differences between us, and the resulting difference in aspects of our oppressions, then what do you do with the fact that the women who clean your houses and tend your children while you attend conferences on feminist theory, are, for the most part, poor and third world women? What is the theory behind racist feminism?

This last question is not completely rhetorical—Lorde wants all of us to examine deeply the prejudices that we carry around and which we inflict on others even in the context of a liberatory movement—such as civil rights or feminism. What is most disturbing to Lorde is that such examination seems to be beyond those who should be the most self-aware—academics engaged in the struggle against sexism.

Lorde also wants to make clear that it is not the responsibility of black feminists to educate white feminists about racism. Just as mainstream feminism engaged in consciousness-raising to realize the ways in which sexism distorted their understandings of themselves and the social world, feminism must do the same kind of soul-searching with regard to racism. Lorde concludes her essay with a call to consciousness:

> Racism and homophobia are real conditions of all our lives in this place and this time: I urge each one of us here to reach down into that deep place of knowledge inside herself and touch that terror and loathing of any difference that lives there. See whose face it wears. Then the personal as political can begin to illuminate all our choices. (*BMCB* 101)

Alice Walker

Alice Walker is popularly known for her fiction, particularly *The Color Purple* that was made into a film in the 1980s. Walker, however, is also an active participant in black feminist criticism. Her book, *In Search of Our Mothers' Gardens* has as its subtitle, 'Womanist Prose'. Walker defines 'womanist' in ways that are very specific to black women's experiences. Her definition of the term even relies upon the every-day dialogue of black mother and their female children:

> Womanist. 1. From womanish. (opp. of 'girlish' i.e. frivolous, irresponsible, not serious). A black feminist or feminist of color. From the black folk expression of mother to female children, 'You acting womanish' i.e. like a woman. Usually referring to audacious, courageous or wilful behaviour. Wanting to know more and in greater depth than is considered 'good' for one. Interesting in grown-up doings. Acting grown-up. Being grown-up. Interchangeable with another black folk expression: 'You trying to be grown.' Responsible. In charge. Serious. (xi)

Walker adds three sub-definitions to the main one outlined above. A womanist is also one 'who loves other women, sexually and/or non-sexually' (xi) She 'loves music. Loves dance. Loves the moon. *Loves the spirit.* Loves love and found and roundness. Loves struggle. Loves the Folk [black folk]. Loves herself. *Regardless'* (xii). Finally, a womanist 'is to feminist as purple is to lavender' (xii).

The last definition succinctly—if analogically—expresses the key difference between mainstream feminism and black feminism for Walker. Lavender is a muted 'feminine' purple, one that does not assert itself, shout or shock—it is in a sense a flippant species of purple. Purple, in contrast, is a deeper lavender—one that reflects the womanists' profound commitment to herself and to the broader humanization of black women.

In Search of Our Mothers' Gardens

The essay, 'In Search of Our Mothers' Gardens', is both a revision of and extension of Virginia Woolf's *A Room of One's Own* (see above). Like Woolf, Walker attempts to locate the lost voices of female artists in history; however, she differs from Woolf in where she looks for these lost artists. She does not look for novelists hiding under the pen-name 'anon', but rather for those women marginalized by their communities—the Saints—'crazy, loony, pitiful women' that Jean Toomer, in his novel, *Cane*, described. As she writes,

> When the poet Jean Toomer walked through the South in the early twenties he discovered a curious thing: black women whose spirituality was so intense, so deep, so *unconscious*, that they were themselves unaware of the richness they held. They stumbled blindly through their lives: creatures so abused and mutilated in body, so dimmed and confused by pain, that they considered themselves unworthy of hope. In the self-less abstractions their bodies became to the men who used them, they become more than 'sexual objects'… they became 'Saints'. (232)

While Toomer sees these women as empty, tragic women, Walker rejects this interpretation and instead forwards the thesis that these women—because of their deep spirituality, and their ability to transcend their circumstances—were the lost artists. These artists might not have 'created' in the traditional sense, but the spirit of creation was restlessly held within all of them:

> For these grandmothers and mothers of ours were not Saints, but Artists, driven to a numb and bleeding madness by the springs of creativity for which there was no release. They were Creators, who lived lives of spiritual waste, because they were so rich in spirituality—which is the basis of Art—that the strain of enduring their unused and unwanted talent drove them insane. (233)

In *A Room of One's Own*, Woolf remarked that a woman with Shakespeare's genius living in Shakespeare's time would have undoubtedly 'gone mad,' for, as she puts it, 'who can measure the heat and violence of a poet's heart when caught and tangled in a woman's body'? (50) Walker comes to a similar conclusion about her 'Saints/Artists'—unable to express themselves, they would have been crazed by their profound frustration. But, while Woolf believes that her 'Saint/Artists, her 'Judith Shakespeares' produced nothing, that their lives were wasted, Walker continues to search and indeed finds their 'art', even of women who did not have Woolf's required conditions for the creation of art—a room of one's own and money. To discover this art, however, Walker realizes that one must not only look 'high'—at bookshelves or the walls of museums—but both 'high' and 'low'. Discussing the experience of her own mother, Walker writes:

> Whatever she planted grew as if by magic, and her fame as a grower of flowers spread over three counties. Because of her creativity with her flowers, even my memories of poverty were seen through a screen of blooms—sunflowers, petunias, roses, dahlias … And I remember people coming to my mother's yard to be given cuttings from her flowers; I hear again the praise showered on her because whatever rocky soil she landed on, she turned into a garden. (241)

For Walker, Woolf's error in *A Room of One's* Own is that she only looked for proof of creativity in the most conventional places—on bookshelves, or on museum walls. What Walker accomplishes in this essay is to expand the definition of art to encompass so-called 'low' forms—her mother's garden, for example, or the eighteenth-century quilt, sewn by a black female slave, that now hangs at the Smithsonian. For Walker and for the women she considers art is a part their daily experience; it is what allows them to survive and which survives after them as a testament to what was both realizable and not realizable given the conditions of their existence.

Patricia Hill Collins

Writing in 1990, Patricia Hill Collins had the privilege of having almost a twenty-year vantage point from which to assess the progress of black feminist thought. In her book *Black Feminist Thought*, Collins articulates some of the advantages and disadvantages of what she calls an 'afrocentric epistemology'—a way of thinking centred on the experiences of black women.

Defining Black Feminist Thought

Collin's exploration of contents and range of black feminist thought begins, sensibly enough, with an attempt at definition. She is particularly interested in whether black feminism is simply the domain of black women, or whether it is an epistemology that can be used and embraced by other men and women of colour as well as white feminists. Also, Collins asks whether being a black women is necessarily enough to generate a black feminist standpoint? This question implicitly critiques the Combahee River Collective's statement (see above) that seems to assume that as a black woman one would necessarily be a black feminist. This kind of thinking, for Collins, equates black feminism with the experiences of black women: her query asks if this equation is sustainable or correct.

Investigating the nature of black feminism, Collins identifies several key dimensions of a black women's standpoint that may or may not develop into a feminist consciousness. In brief, these core themes are an attention to and protest against 'denigrated images of Black woman-hood'; 'black women's activism as mothers, teachers and Black community leaders, and … sensitivity to sexual politics' (Collins 23). Although Collins argues that all black women have, in some form or another, confronted these themes—they have been harassed as black women; they have had to advocate for their children in poorly-financed schools, and so on—this does not necessarily mean that they have translated this experience into a feminist consciousness. As she writes,

> Diversity among Black women produces different concrete experiences that in turn shape various reactions to the core themes. For example, when faced with stereotypical, controlling images of black women, some women—such as Sojourner Truth—demand, 'ain't I a woman'? … In contrast other women internalize the controlling images and come to believe that they are the stereotypes. (Collins 23)

It is clear for Collins that experience alone does not result in feminist consciousness. Black feminism has, in fact, its origin in the confluence of the two—experience that produces consciousness. Experience constitutes a particular historical and social location—a standpoint—from which a feminist consciousness gains its personally and socially persuasive power. For Collins, understanding the origins of feminist consciousness demands understanding the particular standpoints from which this consciousness emerges:

> Black feminist thought consists of theories or specialized thought produced by African-American women intellectuals designed to express a Black women's standpoint. The dimensions of this standpoint include the presence of characteristic core themes, the diversity of Black women's experiences in encountering these core themes, the varying expressions of Black women's Afrocentric feminist consciousness regarding the core women's experiences, consciousness and actions. (Collins 32)

Even though Collins stresses the standpoint of black women, she is keen to expand Black feminism to include the experiences of other women and men. One key component of an 'Afrocentric' epistemology is the uniting of theory and practice—a requirement that has resonance not only for Black women but other groups as well. While other groups may not be able to 'produce black feminist thought' because of their unique standpoints in divergent positions of class, race, sex, and sexuality, the methodology of black feminist thought is transposable to different identity-contexts. The attention paid to the specificity of identities promotes what for Collins is the *sine qua non* of Black feminist thought—a 'humanist vision of community'—one that celebrates and recognizes difference rather than universalizing the experiences of one group to all others.

French Feminism

French feminism developed at about the same time as Anglo-American feminism during the late 1960s and 1970s. Its methodology and concerns, however, were significantly different. While Anglo-American feminism is primarily concerned with the material, ideological and institutional structures of women's oppression—from the boardroom to the bedroom—French feminism uses existing theories of the unconscious, language and materialism to understand women's oppression. Thus, French feminism can be understood as a rewriting of such theorists as Sigmund Freud, Karl Marx, Jacques Lacan, Ferdinand de Saussure, from the perspective of the female, tackling such issues as conceptions of the body, gender, work, and language. Indeed, one of French feminism's primary aims was to instantiate an *'écriture feminine'*—writing by women from the physical and psychological space of 'woman'— in other words, a language of the female body.

Luce Irigaray

Luce Irigaray is perhaps the most clearly antagonistic to traditional psychoanalytic theories of the female body. Her text, *This Sex Which is Not One*, is a repudiation of Freudian understandings of human sexuality—a sexuality that privileges the male body as the site of sexual and psychological satisfaction for both men and women, a mode of thinking called phallocentrism (centrality of the phallus). In phallocentric thought, maleness is the norm against which women's sexuality and anatomy are judged as necessarily abnormal. Because women do not possess a penis, their sexuality is characterized by a lack or absence—and this absence not only affects them physically but psychologically as well. Sigmund Freud's text 'Femininity' is the clearest articulation of phallocentric thinking. In one particular section, Freud describes the profound psychological trauma that accompanies the little girl's realization that she is without a penis and therefore 'castrated':

> The castration complex of girls is ... started by the sight of the genitals of the other sex. They at once notice the difference and, it must be admitted, its significance too. They feel seriously wronged, often declare that they want to 'have something like it too', and fall a victim to 'envy for the penis', which will leave ineradicable traces on their development and the formation of their character and which will not be surmounted in even the most favourable cases without a severe expenditure of psychical energy. (*Femininity* 353)

The female, in Freud's conception, is doomed to a lifetime of unsatisfied sexual and psychological yearning for a penis—or its incarnation in a male child. A woman is also doomed to 'perversion' if she does not accept the passivity of her role in the heterosexual sexual relationship: this passivity involves embracing her sexuality as wholly dependent upon the male. Female masturbation, in Freud's view, is only a pathetic and psychically stunting form of male sexual mimesis; the girl who can not renounce masturbation will never embrace her 'natural' female role as wife, and eventually mother to a male child (the embodiment of her long wished-for penis). Predictably, Freud sees an obstinate retreat into clitoral (active) female sexuality as a prime determinant of female homosexuality in later life. The castration complex, ironically, can only be overcome by the woman embracing her own castration—relishing it as a vehicle towards eventual motherhood.

While such a description of feminine sexuality is objectionable to a twenty-first century audience, it was the predominant understanding of normal female sexuality until feminists challenged it beginning in the 1970s. Irigaray's repudiation of Freud's narratives consists in positing a 'vulva-centric' model of female sexuality to oppose Freud's phallocentric understanding. Rejecting the singularity of phallocentric sexuality—and its focus on the oneness of the penis—Irigaray privileges the plural nature of female sexuality, particularly the erotic possibilities of the vulva and its components—especially the labia. As she writes,

> [W]oman's autoeroticism is very different from man's. He
> needs an instrument in order to touch himself: his hand, wom-
> an's genitals, language—And this stimulation requires a mini-
> mum of activity. But a woman touches herself by and within
> herself directly, without mediation, and before any distinction
> between activity and passivity is possible. A woman 'touches'
> herself' constantly without anyone being able to forbid her
> to do so, for her sex is composed of two lips which embrace
> continually. Thus, within herself she is already two—but not
> divisible into ones—who stimulate each other. (*New French
> Feminisms* 100)

Irigaray's stress on the doubleness of women's sexual nature is a
rejection of the mono-sexuality of phallocentrism. It also allows her
to reject Freudian arguments that women's sexuality is defined by a
lack or an absence: for Irigaray, it is, on the contrary, always multiple
and always independent. Her analysis accomplishes an inversion of
needs—it is not woman who requires man (in fact, he does nothing
but violate her always present sexuality and self-stimulation) it is he
that requires her.

Irigaray's discussion of female sexuality functions as a broader
commentary on male patterns of thinking, particularly on Occidental
epistemology in which the individual is privileged over the collective. Women's multiplicity—her doubleness—is a somatic critique
of this hegemony of the individual. So far away is the female in
Irigaray's conception from this kind of thinking that she resists any
kind of naming or categorization:

> Whence the mystery that she [woman] represents in a cul-
> ture that claims to enumerate everything, cipher everything
> by units, inventory everything by individualities. *She is nei-
> ther one nor two.* She cannot, strictly speaking, be determined
> either as one person or as two. She renders any definition
> inadequate. Moreover she has no 'proper' name. (*New French
> Feminisms* [*NFF*] 101)

Given that woman cannot 'fit' into the cartography of male thought, she can not be expected to communicate in ways that are understandable to those caught within a patriarchal mindset. Thus the typically male disparagement of women's thinking as confused, irrational or superstitious is simply a lack of imagination: women's thinking is only irrational if understood within a rigid paradigm of linear (phallocentric) thought. Women, then, can never say what 'they mean' because their meaning cannot be understood within a male-defined tradition of thought. As Irigaray explains,

> It is therefore useless to trap women into giving an exact defi-nition of what they mean, to make them repeat (themselves) so the meaning will be clear. They have turned back within themselves, which does not mean the same thing as 'within yourself.' They do not experience the same interiority that you do and which perhaps you mistakenly presume they share. 'Within themselves' means in *the privacy of this silent, diffuse tact*. If you ask them insistently what they are thinking about, they can only reply: nothing. Everything. (*NFF* 103)

At first glance, Irigaray may seem to rescue women from male judgments by making the basis of these judgments irrelevant to women's experience. For how can one be blamed for not speaking a language one has never learned? In this repudiation of male thought, however, Irigaray falls into a dangerous trap—the linking of biology with destiny. The irrationality of women has been tied to the irrationality of their bodies for thousands of years, beginning with Plato's theory of the wandering womb.[1] Irigaray simply reaffirms this essentialism in her celebration of women's somatic and hence psychological irrationality. In so doing, she conforms to a thought process that links the mind to

---

1   Aretaios, an ancient Greek physician, famously noted that a woman's womb was 'an animal within an animal'. If it were deprived of a child, it would wander about the body searching for sexual satisfaction, eventually leading to insanity. This theory of the wandering womb was first espoused by Hippocrates and his fol-lowers in Ancient Greece. For more information, click on the following web-link: http://www.classics.uwaterloo.ca/labyrinth/womb.htm. Also, see Mark J. Adair's article 'Plato's View of the Wandering Uterus' in *The Classical Journal* Vol. 91, No. 2 (Dec., 1995 – Jan., 1996), pp. 153–163.

the body, and in this way, she is an unwitting participant in an ancient lineage of essentialist and misogynistic thought.

Hélène Cixous

Hélène Cixous' work is, in many ways, a re-articulation of Simone de Beauvoir's far-reaching critique of Western epistemology (see above). Like Beauvoir, Cixous finds the binarisms that structure Western thought—self/other, man/woman—to be the source of women's continued oppression. Her contention is that this binary epistemology has as its enabling myth the notion of an active male and a passive female. In 'The Newly Born Woman' Cixous notes that

> thought has always worked through opposition,
>
> Speaking/Writing
>
> Parole/Ecriture
>
> High/Low. . .
>
> Organization by hierarchy makes all conceptual organiza-
> tions subject to man. Male privilege, shown in the opposition
> between activity and passivity, which he uses to sustain him-
> self. Traditionally, the question of sexual difference is treated
> by coupling it with the opposition: activity/passivity. (*The
> Hélène Cixous Reader* [*HCR*] 38)

Influenced by the linguistic theories of Jacques Derrida and Jacques Lacan[1], Cixous believed that human experience and thought was wholly constituted through language. As Derrida once famously said, 'there is no outside of the text' ('il n'y'a pas d'hors du texte') by which he meant that there is no 'truth' or reality outside of what is created by and through language. In his introduction to the *Hélène Cixous Reader*, Derrida remarks that Cixous was a master of uncovering the connotations of language—she made language 'speak' those secrets that lay hidden within familiar idioms or phrases. As he notes, 'She [Cixous] knows how to make it [language] say what it keeps in reserve, which in the process also makes it come out of its reserve' (*HCR* vii).

---

1 For a detailed overview of Jacques Derrida and Jacques Lacan, see *An Introduction to Critical Theory*, also available through Humanities E-books.

For Cixous, it is only through language that women can break the binarisms that have condemned them to the negative side of this persistent duality. This language can not by necessity be of the old type—it must break through the male-dominated privileging of linear, rational argument (logocentrism) and instantiate a new kind of writing and hence, thinking. Cixous names her new model of writing '*écriture feminine*' or feminine writing. What, however, makes feminine writing feminine? How does it differ from the everyday writing of both men and women? In answering this implied question, Cixous reveals her indebtedness to psychoanalytic theory—particularly the way in which the language of the body (its desires, its sex, its reproductive capability) is always already inscribed in writing. *Écriture feminine* simply makes the language of the body clearly legible—it refuses, as traditional (log-ocentric) writing does, to silence the body in the act of writing:

> Cixous stresses that the inscription of the rhythms and articu-lations of the mother's body which continue to influence the adult self provides a link to the pre-symbolic union between self and m/other, and so affects the subject's relationship to language, the other, himself [sic] and the world. (*HCR* xxix)

Although '*écriture feminine*' is available to both sexes, Cixous clearly views women as the most able practitioners of this writing. Because women are always already other in a masculine linguistic/philosophical economy, they are necessarily more attuned to this otherness and able, hence, to incorporate it into their writing. To write from the body is necessarily to write the 'other' since the body, in traditional philosophy, is that which is rejected in the formation of 'rational' thought.[1]

---

1   One has only to read Plato's 'Allegory of the Cave' and/or 'Symposium' to under-stand that the path to knowledge in his philosophy is predicated on the rejection of the sensual and the senses. In 'The Allegory of the Cave', for example, those who are to become philosophers must escape the 'cave' that is an allegorical representation of 'the prison house of sight (senses)'. To read 'The Allegory of the Cave' and the 'Symposium' click on the following link: http://bartleby.com/ and search for both titles in the search tool provided.

The Laugh of the Medusa

In this essay, Cixous articulates fully her concept of the *'écriture feminine'*. She argues that within a male (phallologocentric) paradigm of writing, woman has no voice. In order to understand this contention, we must unpack more fully the word 'phallologocentric'. This neologism is a convenient shorthand for Derridean and Lacanian views about the relationship of language to gender and culture. Lacan noted that the structure of language is predicated upon the entry of the subject into the paternal world (the symbolic); it is this entry that confers systemization upon the subject's language.[1] The Symbolic's nucleus—its ordering structure—is the phallus. Hence, traditional writing is always phallocentric because it is predicated upon the Symbolic, which always already, in its very structure, privileges the Phallus. Cixous adds the word 'logos' to phallocentric to signal traditional writing's privileging of speech over writing. This hierarchization is what Derrida points to in much of his philosophy; he argues, in fact, that linguistic structure always implies a celebration of speech over writing, primarily because writing produces a text that is subject to a variety of interpretations—its meanings proliferate. Thus, the logos—the word—is celebrated over the text; hence, male thought is phallologocentric at its core—even, ironically, when thought is expressed in writing.

Understandably, a woman's voice can hardly be heard in this context *as a woman's voice*. Women can only write themselves if they find a way of reclaiming their unique sexuality in this context. But the context itself deems their sexuality as irredeemably other, and as such, as indefinable within a phallologocentric paradigm. As Cixous notes,

> It is impossible to define a feminine practice of writing, and this is an impossibility that will remain, for this practice can never be theorized, enclosed, coded, which doesn't mean that

---

1 As noted in *An Introduction to Critical Theory*, 'the Symbolic realm, like Freud's superego, functions as the ordering structure for the unconscious. It is the linguistically-based mechanism for the articulation of the 'I' [the individual's identity] and for the elements of the unconscious that constitute the 'I' and its relationship to the world around it' (Rich, *An Introduction to Critical Theory*, 48).

it doesn't exist. But it will always surpass the discourse that regulates the phallocentric system; it does and will take place in areas other than those subordinated to the philosophico-the-oretical domination. It will be conceived of only by subjects who are breakers of automatism, by peripheral figures that no authority can ever subjugate. (Cixous)

So, what is Cixous' answer to this quandary? Should women write, and if so, how? Cixous believes that in order to write as a woman, women, in general, must reclaim their sexuality—one that is female-centered and which celebrates their own sources of pleasure, distinct from men. Women's writing must issue from this site of *jouissance* (pleasure, delight). If women are able to do so, they will of necessity establish a new signifying system—one that displaces the phallologocentrism that has dominated their writing lives. Cixous believes in fact that the destruction of binary thought (good/bad, man/woman) can only occur through '*l'écriture feminine*'.

Cixous' 'mascot' for *l'écriture feminine* is the mythical figure of Medusa.[1] For Cixous, Medusa's power resides in her essential repu-diation of the binary system: she is both male and female. The snakes that constitute her 'hair' are, in Cixous' reading, a plethora of phal-luses. The sight of this symbolic destruction of binary phallologocen-tric thought is what makes Medusa so terrifying to men—rendering them stones (hence) speechless, and also what makes her so empow-ering to women.

Cixous, however, does not want to leave men out of the potentiali-ties of *l'écriture feminine*. She believes that men are hampered also by the strictures of phallologocentric thought, particularly because such thought prevents them from understanding and hearing a woman's 'true' voice. L*'écriture feminine* is thus an opportunity for both sexes to remove the blinders of dichotomous thinking, and, via a privileg-ing of non-phallic-centered sexuality to see subjectivity instead of otherness.

---

1 Medusa was a woman with beautiful hair who was raped by Poseidon in Athena's temple. As punishment for the crime of being raped (!), Athena turned Medusa's hair into snakes. After this, any man who saw Medusa would be turned into stone. Medusa was decapitated by Perseus.

Monique Wittig

Monique Wittig entered the conversation about women, writing, the sex/gender system in a distinct manner from the theorists we consider above. Although she was an active member of the women's liberation movement in France in the 1960s and 1970s even collaborating on a widely disseminated manifesto, her most profound interrogation of the sex/gender system occurred through her fiction—in particular, her two novels, *Les guérillères* (The Woman Warriors) and *L'Corps lesbienne* (The Lesbian Body).[1] Writing about her composing process, Wittig remarks on her desire to disrupt traditional (male-defined) linearity in her fiction and to instantiate a new aesthetics that embraces the feminine, one that necessarily rejects the singularity (phallocentric discourse) for fragmentariness and plurality:

> The book (*Les guérillères*) is composed of fragments distributed in three parts; each part is preceded by a thick circle in the centre of a white page....The constitutive element [of the novel] is the pronoun, the plural personal pronoun of the third person, **elles**. It is utilized like a character. Ordinarily, a character of a novel represents a singular entity. But here from the start a collective entity developed in the literary workshop and took over all the space of the narrative. (*On Monique Wittig* [*OMG*]38)

In *Les guérillères*, Wittig interrupts the linear narrative by graphics and random names that pepper the text. Most importantly, she refuses the singularity of a character by creating a plural community as character—the elles that are the woman warriors and that wage a furious epic war against the patriarchy that surrounds them. Wittig describes the narrative as follows:

> In the first part, **elles** has already turned the world upside down. The war belongs to the past. **Elles** tries to make its way across the labyrinth of a dead culture of ancient signs, of rep-

---

1 Wittig is also the author of *L'Opoponax* which won the Prix Medicis in 1964. Although revolutionary in its subject matter, it is a less obvious example of the ideology that Wittig forwards in *The Lesbian Body* and *Les guérillères*.

resentations ... **Elles** exalts itself in some of the 'feminaries'. (*OMW* 41–42)

What Wittig achieves in *Les guérillères* is a vulva-centric discourse—one that rejects singularity and privileges the female. Yet, it is wrong to conceptualize this vulva-centric discourse as simply an uninspired inversion of phallocentrism. For vulva-centrism deploys its own narcissistic icons in order to topple them eventually. In this passage of *Les guérillères* **elles** engages in a discourse of non-exaltation of their bodies—in so doing, it employs a rhetoric of *paraleipsis* or suggestion by omission.[1]

> The women say that they perceive their bodies in their entirety. They say that they do not favour any of its parts on the grounds that it was formerly a forbidden object. They say that they do not want to become prisoners in their own ideology. They say that they did not garner and develop symbols that were necessary to them at an earlier period to demonstrate their strength. For example they do not compare the vulvas to the sun moon stars. They do not say that the vulvas are like black suns in the shining light. (58)

In this passage, Wittig is engaging in a double discourse—she both celebrates the rejection of particularity and singularity that characterizes a non-phallocentric discourse, and also suggests the potential dangers of such celebration; the deification of other parts of the body. Thus the sentence 'they do not say that the vulvas are like black suns in the shining light' is a celebration that deconstructs itself by its own implicit paraleiptic denial.

Wittig is more provocative in the novel that follows *Les guérillères*, *Le Corps Lesbien,* commonly described as a love letter from an Amazon to a lover. This novel is also an extraordinarily intimate exploration of the notion of the 'lesbian' and the 'body'—a coupling

---

1 A good definition of paraleipsis is 'a pretended or apparent omission; a figure by which a speaker artfully pretends to pass by what he really mentions; as, for example, if an orator should say, "I do not speak of my adversary's scandalous venality and rapacity, his brutal conduct, his treachery and malice."' (*Webster's Dictionary*)

that Wittig called a paradox in her discussion of this novel. The paradoxical nature of this coupling is more apparent because body is 'masculine' in French and the word *lesbien*, of course, only applies to women and a woman-centered sexuality. So to speak of a lesbian body is to challenge—both linguistically and ideologically—conventional patriarchal notions of the body. As Wittig explains,

> [L]esbian by its proximity to [the word] 'body' seemed to me to destabilize the general notion of the body. It's a good way for make to make you understand that a writer writes word by word, each word being a material entity as well as a conceptual one. (*OMG* 46)

The body in this novel is never conceptualized (w)holistically; it is persistently described in parts, and each part is explored by the fractured 'I' of the text in a sometimes disturbing, sometimes comforting duet of intimacy. The body is also celebrated in its timeliness—it is not conceptualized as paralyzed in youth, but in a constant process of aging and decomposition:

> The gleam of your teeth your joy your arteries your veins your hollow habitations your organs your nerves their rupture, their spurting forth death slow decomposition stench being devoured by works your open skull, all will be equally unbearable to her. (Wittig 15)

This passage forcefully collapses the emotions and subjectivity of the body. The ego of the 'I'—a singularity that is consistently deconstructed in this text—is violently undone by the hegemony of the body. Le *Corps Lesbien* reverses the mind/body duality—it not only inverts it, but renders such a duality impossible. The mind is the body is the mind is the I and so on. The omission of punctuation precludes the separation of these usually separated parts of the 'self'.

Le Corps Lesbien also compromises the notion of an 'I-you' separation. It rejects this linguistically by creating the neologism of the j/e, translated as 'm/y' in English. Wittig creates this neologism in order to indicate the inseparable oneness of the twoness of the lovers in the novel. Through the '/' separating the m/y (j/e) in the novel,

Wittig challenges the originary binarism of 'the me' and the 'not-me' that structures human experience according to psychoanalysis (both Lacanian and Freudian).

One is Not Born a Woman

Wittig's most famous and controversial theoretical work is her essay, 'One is Not Born a Woman'. This title is an obvious play on Simone de Beauvoir's assertion that 'one is not born a woman; one becomes one' (see above). In typical fashion, Wittig pushes this assertion beyond its original intention and contends that one can only be defined as a 'woman' if one conforms to very narrow ideological boundaries. Thus, any woman that defies the 'woman'-defining boundaries of heterosexuality or motherhood, for example, is not a 'woman' as this category is traditionally understood. To be a 'woman' is, in Wittig's words, to participate in a 'mythic construction … which reinterprets physical features … through the network of relationships in which they are perceived' (*The Critical Tradition* 1639).

Wittig moves on to theorize the possibility of womanness for lesbians given the definitional boundaries of this category. Unsurprisingly, she concludes that 'lesbians are not women'. Wittig is not denying lesbians' biological femininity, rather she is expressing their essential independence from a category in which they—because of their life and love choices—can find no place. The fact that Wittig can state that lesbians are really not 'women' reveals the urgent necessity to expand radically the categories of both men and women. This involves looking carefully at the material networks of oppression—the economic and social reasons that compel 'woman' to be definable only in relation to men. Although Marxism might seem a fruitful site for such an examination, Wittig faults it for its sole focus on 'class' rather than on the intersection of sex and class. As she writes,

> Class consciousness is not enough. We must try to under-
> stand philosophically (politically) these concepts of 'subject
> and 'class consciousness' and how they work in relation to

our history. When we discover that women are the objects of oppression and appropriation, at the very moment that we become able to perceive this, we become subjects in the sense of cognitive subjects. (*The Critical Tradition* 1642)

In this passage, Wittig is anxious to free women's experience from encapsulation in other forms of oppression—class, race and so on. She desires to return to women the individuality of their experience and in so doing put into question the sex/gender system that operates under a variety of different contexts—in both the bourgeoisie and the proletariat. Wittig applauds Frederick Engels, Marx's co-author and most intimate colleague, for his pioneering recognition of an oppressive sex/gender system in his work *Origins of Family, Private Property and the State* (1884). Wittig, however, wishes to push Engel's analysis further. She does so by using the semiotic 'lesbian' and demonstrating how it is uncapturable within the existing understandings of women. The fact that the category 'woman' cannot apply to the lesbian experience only shows up the former's epistemological limitations as well as the pre-emption of its revolutionary potential. Until and unless the lesbian can be considered a 'woman' no real substantive change can occur in the conditions of women's lives. Wittig concurs with Beauvoir that 'one is not born a woman' but in Wittig's understanding the 'lesbian' is not and can never be a woman within this system.

Julia Kristeva

Like many of the theorists in this volume, Julia Kristeva's work is an amalgamation of several strands of thought: namely, psychoanalysis, semiotics and feminism. (Although it should be noted that Kristeva's feminist credentials have been questioned and re-questioned throughout her career). For our purposes, her work constitutes an important intervention into the thinking of Jacques Lacan and to a lesser extent, Sigmund Freud.[1] Her main critique of both Lacan and Freud is their neglect of the role of the mother in the formation of the

1   For a full discussion of Jacques Lacan, see *An Introduction to Critical Theory*, also available through Humanities E-books.

child's psyche. In order to reintroduce the 'mother' as a significant factor in the child's psychological development, Kristeva rewrites the Lacanian imaginary and mirror-stage by introducing three key concepts: the *chora*, the *semiotic* and the *abject*. These three concepts structure Kristeva's later analysis of the function of 'woman' in establishing the symbolic structure—the 'Law of the Father' as delineated by Lacan. Her most famous work in this regard is 'Stabat Mater', an article that closely considers the role of the Virgin Mary in disabling a discourse of the maternal that escapes traditional Lacanian understandings of the Symbolic. Before reviewing 'Stabat Mater', we will examine Kristeva's rewriting of Lacan's discussion of the imaginary, the symbolic and the mirror stage. We will do so by examining the three concepts she uses to rewrite Lacan: the semiotic, the chora, and the abject.

The Semiotic

In an interview, Kristeva rather startlingly stated that it is impossible to be a woman: 'to believe that one is a "woman" is almost as absurd and obscurantist as to believe that one 'is a "man"' (www.cddc.vt.edu/feminism/kristeva.html). Discussing the *Bible's* 'Book of Ruth' for example, Kristeva points to the 'alterity' that structures Judaism. Ruth is a non-Jew and a foreigner, and yet Ruth ancestrally founds the house of David. Thus, as Kristeva notes, 'at the heart of sovereignty [of the house of David] there is an inscription of foreign femininity. Institutionalized Judaism does not recognize this foreign lineage, yet it is part of a tradition of generosity towards the other that is at the heart of Jewish monotheism' (Kristeva). Even at the moment of its guarantee of sovereignty the figure of woman is inscribed as 'other'—an 'other' that paradoxically (in both of paradox's meaning: contradiction and against orthodoxy) enables the subject. For Kristeva, then, there is no possibility of a positive definition of woman. Woman as a concept is a negative: in Lacanian psychoanalysis, for example, it is the feminine—the woman—that must be repressed in order to fully enter into the 'Symbolic' structure—to fully integrate in Lacan's words, the 'Name-of-the-Father'. For Lacan, this entry into the Symbolic requires that the child forgoes desiring that which is disallowed by the 'Father" as authoritarian concept. The entry to the Symbolic is relatively smooth for those who do not suffer from psychological illnesses, such as psychosis or narcissism. (In Lacan's view, such illnesses are a result of the inability to enter into the symbolic). Kristeva differs from Lacan in her understanding of the process of the psychological integration of the Symbolic on the part of the subject. For Kristeva, the passage to the Symbolic is not so simple or clear-cut. Her notion of the Symbolic contains within it a constant threat to the smooth functioning of the Symbolic: the semiotic. The semiotic is comprised of those pre-oedipal drives and urges that disrupt the Symbolic and that compromise the unproblematic integration of the 'Name-of-the-Father' in the subject's psyche. Unsurprisingly the semiotic is tied to the maternal function in Kristeva's cartography of the unconscious. Whereas for Lacan, the 'mother'—a symbol of the pre-oedipal, pre-symbolic state—is abandoned for the law-giving 'Father', for Kristeva, this abandonment can never be accomplished. Thus, 'Woman' is impossible to define precisely because the notion of 'Woman' depends upon an impossible abandonment of the drives that make up the 'semiotic'.

The Chora

For Kristeva, the 'home' of the semiotic is located in what she calls 'the *chora*'. This name is derived from Greek for 'womb' and is characterized in Plato's *Timaeus* as an entity without form but which 'receives all things and in some mysterious way partakes of the intelligible, and is most incomprehensible' (Moi 161). Kristeva's definition of the 'chora' shares many similarities with Plato's—it is the maternal space that is both 'anterior to and underlies figuration'. The *chora* thus plays two contradictory roles: it refuses signification (entry into the symbolic) at the same time that it guarantees it. In some sense, the *chora* as the pre-oedipal space of maternal plenitude— similar to Lacan's imaginary that precedes the mirror stage—is the necessary staging ground for the Symbolic. Entry into the Symbolic is predicated upon the abandonment of the *chora*. Thus, the Symbolic takes its definition from the exclusion of the *chora*; it is the negative—like 'Woman' that makes possible the positive formation of an ideal of signification—the 'Father' or the Symbolic.

As we have noted, Kristeva, does not believe that this abandonment is attainable. In fact, her methodology of *semanalysis* arises out of an understanding of and commitment to retaining the heterogeneous nature of signifying systems:

> The point is not to replace the semiotics of signifying systems by considerations on the biological code appropriate to the nature of those employing them.... It is rather to postulate the heterogeneity of biological operations in respect of signifying operations and to study the dialectics of the former (*The Kristeva Reader* 30).

Kristeva's Symbolic, then, is not the nice clean arena of logic and rule of law that Lacan's is. It is replete with the semiotic—with those drives and urges that Kristeva views as a constant within the Symbolic.

The Abject

Another aspect of the semiotic that challenges the symbolic is Kristeva's notion of the abject that she developed in her book *Powers of Horror*. The 'abject' seems, at first glance, to be a reworking of Lacan's 'real', but it is closely tied to Kristeva's understanding of the maternal relationship that underlies signification (and threatens it also). As Kristeva explains, 'abjection preserves what existed in the archaism of pre-objectal relationship in the immemorial violence with which body becomes separated from another body in order to be' (*Powers of Horror* 10).

It is a site that threatens the clear-cut boundaries of subject and object such as the way in which the pregnant maternal body interrupts the clear-cut distinction of 'me and you'. The abject, however, is not only associated with the 'archaism' of the maternal relationship but also its opposite: the subject's apprehension of his or her own mortality. It is this aspect of the abject that makes it seem like semiotic refuse, comprised of that which compels repugnance and rejection. The abject, in this sense, may best be apprehended by considering the psychological effects of trauma; for Kristeva, the witnessing of trauma—wounds, death—brings the spectator into an unbearable proximity of the body's uncontrollability—its independence from the subject's control and, by extension, its mortality:

> A wound with blood and pus, or the sickly acrid smell of sweat, of decay, does not signify death. In the presence of signified death—a flat encephalograph [device measuring brain activity] for instance—I would understand, react or accept. No, as in true theatre, without makeup or masks, refuse and corpses *show me* what I permanently thrust aside in order to live. These body fluids, this defilement, this shit are what life withstands, hardly and with difficulty, on the part of death. There, I am at the border of my condition as a living being (*Powers* 3)

Understandably, the abject is necessarily tied to emotions of fear. As such, Kristeva's proposed etiology of phobias in the subject is closely linked to the abject. A phobia, for Kristeva, is a moment of psychological displacement. A fear of cats, for example, is not really a fear of cats in and of themselves, but rather cats trigger a memory of failed separation, of the undecidability of the boundary between subject and object that threatens the integrity of the subject.

Even though the abject is the etiology of fear and phobia; it is also a source of *jouissance* in art. Art's definition, according to Kristeva, partly depends upon its abject-associated *jouissance*, a 'joy' that comes about through catharsis: 'The various means of *purifying* the abject—the various catharses—make up the history of religions, and end up with the catharsis *par excellence* called art, both on the far and near side of religion' (*Powers* 17)

Stabat Mater

'Stabat Mater' is Kristeva's meditation upon the function of the Virgin Mary in the collective psychology of Western (patriarchal) culture. This text is unique because it is, in actuality, two texts. Most of the discussion is divided into two columns: in one column, Kristeva writes about her own experience as a mother; in the other, she analyzes the iconography of the Virgin Mary. In writing about her own experience, Kristeva abandons academic-speak and moves into a discourse of poetic free association. This is in stark contrast to the rhetoric she employs when considering the symbolism of Mary. Here, she adopts the tone of objective analysis. The contrast is even more marked because of the different typefaces that Kristeva uses: her discussion of her maternal body is in bold, while the discussion of the Virgin Mary is in regular typeface. Even though Kristeva rejects the notion of an 'écriture feminine' (a distinctly female writing process) one is tempted to conclude that in writing about herself, she is writing from 'the body' and in writing about the Virgin Mary she is writing from the 'mind'. Thus, the two columns duplicate the dialectic—the constant interchange—between the 'feminine' and the 'masculine'—or, more specifically, the 'semiotic' and the 'symbolic' (although it would be a mistake to equate the semiotic to the feminine in all cases).

Briefly, Kristeva argues that the Virgin Mary plays a paradoxi-cal role in patriarchal (male-centred) thinking around the maternal. As an icon, she both celebrates the maternal while she also allows a needed separation from it. She functions then to disable the threaten-ing potential of the *semiotic* and, by extension, the *chora*, which as we have seen above, is the pre-oedipal space of maternal plenitude—where the child is not independent of the mother. The *chora,* while comforting in some ways, is also threatening because it reminds the subject of the precariousness of his or her independence and integ-rity; the *chora* via the semiotic tries to reassert itself through drives and urges which continually challenge the primacy of the symbolic in the subject's life. For Kristeva, the deification of Mary is predicated upon her disavowal of the maternal function:

> Freedom with respect to the maternal territory then becomes the pedestal upon which love of God is erected…. The resorption of femininity within the Maternal is specific to many civiliza-

tions, but Christianity, in its own fashion, brings it to its peak. Could it be that such a reduction represents no more than masculine appropriation of the Maternal, which, in line with our hypothesis, is only a fantasy masking primary narcissism? (*The Kristeva Reader* [*TKR*] 163)

This primary narcissism is the false belief in the autonomy of the subject from the mother—it is founded upon the rejection of the maternal as part and parcel of the subject's coming to being. For Kristeva, the maternal is never overcome and we are always, in her words, 'subjects in process'. Never free from the originary maternal bond and from the complex semiotic drives that emanate from it, the subject is always in the process of negotiating the symbolic's demands within a complex of semiotic urges. The Virgin Mary's attractiveness as an icon lies in her ability to rescue the subject from the semiotic. While the maternal body is normally a somatic repository of 'the heterogeneity of the signifier' where 'no signifier can uplift it without leaving a remainder', the Virgin Mary is a representation of a tamed 'maternal'. She both embodies the maternal's prerogative over the subject at the same time that she acknowledges the maternal's subservient position to the subject. One of the most important ways that the iconography of the virgin accomplishes this is that she represents

A skilful balance of concessions and constraints involving feminine paranoia, the representation of virgin motherhood appears to crown the efforts of a society to reconcile the social remnants of matrilinearism and the unconscious needs of primary narcissism on the one hand, and on the other, the requirements of a new society based on exchange and before long on increased production, which require the contribution of the superego and rely on the symbolic paternal agency (*TKR* 181–182)

This balance is best seen in the representations of the Virgin and child. Mary's attitude toward Christ—her child and her God—is a complex mixture of masochism, veneration and pride. Writing about the famous nativity scene of Piero della Francesca in London,[1] Kristeva notes that this representation of maternal humility is paired with a feeling of 'gratification and *jouissance*', the latter born of the knowledge that the salvation is hers as well, as mother of God but also 'wife and daughter.' The latter identifications are possible given the knowledge that every mother through their reproductive capability are 'destined to ... Eternity (of the spirit and the species) (*The Kristeva Reader* 172). Kristeva's own autobiographical account that runs alongside her discussion of the Virgin Mary underscores the dialectical nature of the maternal bond. In one entry she writes, for example,

> I yearn for the Law. And since it is not made for me alone, I venture to desire outside the law. Then, narcissism thus awakened—the narcissism that wants to be sex—roams astonished. In sensual rapture, I am distraught. Nothing reassures, for only the law sets anything down. Who calls such suffering *jouissance*? It is the pleasure of the damned. (*TKR* 175)

Here Kristeva makes visible the struggle of the semiotic and the symbolic embodied in the experience of motherhood. She 'yearns for the Law' and yet the narcissism of maternal connectivity (perhaps the *chora)* interrupts the re-absorption (physically and psychologically) of the Law. For Kristeva as mother, 'lucidity'—the rational signifying system of the symbolic—only denies her the imagined plenitude between the child and herself; it, in her words 'would restore her as cut in half, alien to its other ... ' (*TKR* 179).

At the end of this essay, Kristeva posits a reformulation of ethics that would include the maternal experience; she names this ethics, appropriately, '*herethics*'. In this ethics—divorced from a morality that denies the flesh (the semiotics), 'the maternal bond, and love' are affirmed rather than denied, and therefore *herethics* is defined as 'undeath [*a-mort*]' that renders the iconographic necessity of the Virgin—the escape route of the maternal—unnecessary and irrelevant.

---

1   To view the Francesca painting referenced above, click on the following link:
    http://www.wga.hu/frames-e.html?/html/p/piero/francesc/nativity.html

Materialist Feminism

Materialist feminism uses the theoretical contributions of nineteenth and twentieth century thinkers to understand the mechanics of the oppression of women. One of its first practitioners was Gayle Rubin, who in her seminal article, 'The Traffic in Women: Notes on the Political Economy of Sex', adopted and transformed the theories of Karl Marx, Sigmund Freud, Jacques Lacan and Claude Lèvi-Strauss to understand the formation and reproduction of what she calls 'the sex/gender system'. Similarly, Gayatri Chakrovarty Spivak uses the work of Marx, Jacques Derrida and Gilles Deleuze to unpack the meaning of subalternity in reference to women's experience in India and elsewhere. We will first consider Gayle Rubin's article and then turn to Spivak.

Gayle Rubin

The Traffic in Women: Notes on the Political Economy of Sex

Published in 1975, Gayle Rubin's article is both a response to radical feminism's theorizing of women's oppression and a departure point for more theoretically inflected analyses of the 'woman question'. Finding many of radical feminism's explanations for women's oppression unsatisfactory—especially ones that claimed the existence of prehistoric matriarchies overthrown by a patriarchal revolution or the more essentialist explanation of innate male aggression as the reason for women's oppression—Rubin searches for an understanding of women's situation that highlights the situatedness of women within certain social relations of production and reproduction. For this she is indebted to Karl Marx, who, in his discussion of class structures, insisted upon an analysis that acknowledges the historical specificity of class and labour arrangements. Asking 'what are [the] relationships by which a female becomes an oppressed women', Rubin takes Marx's brief discussion of the ontology of capital as capital as a theoretical template for organizing her own initial discussion:

> Marx once asked: 'what is a Negro slave? A man of the black race. The one explanation is as good as the other. A Negro is a Negro. He only becomes a slave in certain relations. A cotton spinning Jenny is a machine for spinning cotton. It becomes *capital* only in certain relations. Torn from these relationships it is no more capital than gold in itself is money or sugar is the price of sugar'. (*The Second Wave* [*TSW*] 28)

Inserting women into this passage, Rubin arrives at the following formulation:

> What is a domesticated woman? A female of the species. The one explanation is as good as the other. A woman is a woman. She only becomes a domestic, a wife, a chattel, a playboy bunny, a prostitute, or a human dictaphone in certain relations. Torn from these relationships she is no more the helpmate of man than gold in itself is money … etc. (*TSW 28*)

Having established that the oppression of women is not a natural biological fact, but rather emanates from certain relationships into which the woman is placed, Rubin returns to the question articulated above—i.e. from where do these relationships arise that define woman as 'man's helpmate' or 'chattel' and so on? In short, what is the social and cultural aetiology for the oppression of women? And what social and political purpose does it serve?

To investigate these questions, Rubin, an anthropologist by training, understandably turns to the most influential anthropologist of the twentieth century, Claude Lévi-Strauss. Lévi-Strauss aimed to concretize the Saussure's identification of the 'grammar' of culture—its underlying logic—within his anthropological investigations of human culture. Rubin finds his discussion of kinship systems enormously useful for her project. Lévi-Strauss's investigation of kinship systems was one of the first to consider closely the role of women in the establishment of kinship networks and in the origins of the incest-taboo. He found that women, among other 'gifts' must 'circulate' in order for certain social networks to be developed:

> Your own mother, your own sister, your own pigs, your own yams that you have piled up you may not eat. Other people's mothers, other people's sisters, other people's pigs, other people's yams that they have piled up, you may eat. (*TSW* 35)

The incest taboo and the gift imperative are closely related. In order to establish social networks that will be of material and social benefit, human beings, animals and food must be circulated—must be exchanged—as gifts. Thus, to 'consume' one's own mother, sister, daughter is to fall outside of this social network and to threaten one's social and economic viability. The question still arises, however, why women? Why must women be the ones to circulate—to be consumed by another—and not men? According to Lévi-Strauss, marriage—however this is defined in a particular culture—is the most 'basic form of gift exchange, in which ... women ... are the most precious of gifts' (*TSW* 36). The exchange of women leads to familial alliances between men that assist both families in their economic viability. The following quotation—crude as it is—helps us to understand the utility of this exchange in ensuring the founding and continuation of beneficial male alliances:

> 'What woman,' mused a young Northern Melpa man,[1] 'is ever strong enough to get up and say "Let us make *moka*, let us find wives and pigs, let us give our daughters to men, let us wage war, let us kill our enemies!" 'No indeed not! ... they are little rubbish things who stay at home, simply, don't you see'? (*TSW* 37)

Thus, marriage ensures that men will have the alliances they need to wage war, hunt, and so on. It also ensures that a certain division of labour between the sexes obtains—one that helps to define the social roles of the different sexes: their gender. Rubin insists on the wording 'sex/gender' system in order to emphasize the importance

---

1   Melpa is located in Papua, New Guinea.

of understanding how sex—biological femaleness—becomes a gender—a social and political position of power (or the lack of it) within certain relationships.

To understand how this division of the sexes continues to operate in the collective psyche of 'modern' societies, Rubin turns to Sigmund Freud. She remarks at the compatibility of Lévi-Strauss's theories of kinship systems and Freud's theories of female development. As she writes,

> The precision of the fit between Freud and Lévi-Strauss is striking. Kinship systems require a division of sexes. The Oedipal phase divides the sexes. Kinship systems include sets of rules governing sexuality. The Oedipal crisis is the assimilation of these rules and taboos. Compulsory heterosexuality is the product of kinship. The Oedipal phase constitutes heterosexual desire. Kinship rests on a radical difference between the rights of men and women. The Oedipal complex confers male rights upon the boy and forces the girl to accommodate herself to her lesser rights. (*TSW* 51)

In some sense, then, psychoanalysis is the psycho-social internalization and rationalization of patriarchal kinship systems. It confers upon the male role, signified by the phallus (the symbolic power of the penis), the necessary power to compel assent to a system of exchange that benefits men. A widely-practiced symbolic shorthand for this exchange of women is the custom of the father 'giving away' the bride to the groom in traditional marriage ceremonies. This act symbolizes not only the gift of the bride but also the alliance that this gift creates between these two men and their families.

Rubin's title—the traffic in women—articulates the conclusion that she arrives at with regard to the aetiology of women's oppression. Women are not oppressed as an inevitable result of their biology, but because of their role in a social system that demands their exchange in order to establish alliances between men. This hypothesis clarifies the compulsoriness of heterosexuality—to refuse to be a party to this exchange is a social and economic loss to men and necessitates that other women be found to take the place of the lesbian woman.

In this article, Rubin develops a political economy of women much as Marx developed a political economy of capitalism in his work, *Capital*. Rubin, like Marx, does not look for the source of women's oppression in just one social sector; rather she understands that the sources of social stratification are numerous and overlapping, and must be untangled in order to develop an apprehension of the modes of production and reproduction of oppressive dynamics (whether they involve women, men, or other social groups).

Gayatri Chakravorty Spivak

Gayatri Chakravorty Spivak is perhaps one of the most intellectually far-reaching postcolonial critics working today. Her work demands a profound understanding of Western philosophy, critical theory, history, and language. As a student of Jacques Derrida and translator of one of his most important works, *On Grammatology*, Spivak's work owes much of its intellectual rigor to deconstruction, but her own analyses range far beyond this theoretical paradigm to interrogate that which remains unquestioned in even the most 'radical' of critical theory, namely, the notion of transparency (that which is self-evident, obvious, and therefore requiring no explication), the 'knowing' subject, and most importantly, 'the subaltern'.

Can the Subaltern Speak?

Her most widely anthologized essay, 'Can the Subaltern Speak'? is a virtuoso interrogation of Western (imperialist) understandings of the 'subject', the 'intellectual's' political positioning, capitalism, and, of course, the 'subaltern'. Spivak's definition of the subaltern is subtle and demands an understanding of her critique of the subject formation in Western thought, as well as her complex decoding of the notion of representation in Marx's work, particularly, the *Eighteenth Brumaire of Louis Napoleon*.

The first part of her article spotlights a discussion between two intellectual giants of critical theory: Michel Foucault and Gilles Deleuze. While both of these theorists interrogate the notion of the all-knowing subject (the *cogito)* introduced by Rene Descartes, Spivak critiques them for not extending this discussion into questions of ideology and its implication in the formation of their own critiques of the subject. She thus points to an unnerving contradiction in their own intellectual work; while Deleuze (and his co-author Felix Guattari) are concerned with the psychological etiologies of revolutionary movements (their sustaining desire), their discussion of such movement's participants is hopelessly totalizing—they do not bother to explain the salient differences between the revolutionary subjects they discuss. In fact, as Spivak points out, they simply refer to 'the workers' struggle' as constituting 'a diffuse mass'. Critiquing this characterization, Spivak calls attention to the potential dangers in such totalizing gestures—even if such gestures are, as she implies, 'innocent' of obfuscating intent:

> The invocation of *the* workers' struggle is baleful in its very innocence; it is incapable of dealing with global capitalism: the subject-production of worker and unemployed with nation-state ideologies in its Centre; the increasing subtraction of the working class in the Periphery from the realization of surplus-value and thus from 'humanistic' training in consumerism; and the large-scale presence of paracapitalist labour as well as the heterogeneous structural status of agriculture in the Periphery. Ignoring the international division of labour; rendering 'Asia' (and on occasion 'Africa') transparent (unless the subject is ostensibly the 'Third World') … these are problems as common to much poststructuralist as to structuralist theory. (*Colonial Discourse and Postcolonial Theory*[*CDPT*] 67)

More problematic than just this broad brush-stroke approach to 'the third world' and to 'the worker's struggle' is Deleuze and Foucault's seeming blindness to their own subject-positions as intellectuals in the first world. Their under-theorizing of the specificity of their location in regards to 'power' and its application either through intellectual or material capital is most disturbing, for Spivak, because it emanates from theoreticians who have supposedly considered very closely the workings of power in the formation of ideologies and identity (see the Foucault discussion above). In part, this omission stems from a general problematic that Spivak locates—the refusal (or inability) to articulate a theory of interests within an analysis of power relations. This failure is discernable within the subtle elisions that occur in Deleuze and Foucault's discussion of power. As Spivak notes, desire becomes conflated with subjectivity, 'the individual' and power; thus, their critique of the Cartesian subject—the subject that transcends the networks of power and ideology is reconstituted as the transparent 'Subject of theory', as transcendent and untheorized as Descartes' *cogito*:[1]

> The failure of Deleuze and Guattari to consider the relations between desire, power and subjectivity renders them incapable of articulating a theory of interests. In this context, their indifference to ideology (a theory of which is necessary for understanding of interests) is striking but consistent. Foucault's commitment to 'genealogical' speculation prevents him from locating, in 'great names' like Marx or Freud, watersheds in some continuous stream of intellectual history. This commitment has created an unfortunate resistance in Foucault's work to 'mere' ideological critique. (*CDPT* 68)

Spivak notes that the 'unquestioned valorisation' of the oppressed as subject leads not to an overturning of oppressive ideologies and (the consequent) inequitable division of labour, but rather to their reification. For Spivak, Foucault and Deleuze's blindness to their own implication in the reconsolidation of the international division of labour—a division wherein the disenfranchised within the 'third world' (for lack of a better term) is subject to the demands of first world capital interests—only further prevents the articulation of a meaningful discourse that would interrogate and problematise the division of labour and the ideological constitution of a 'third world'. As she rhetorically demands, 'what happens to the critique of the

---

1 For Deleuze and Guattari's understanding of the implication of desire in power, see Gilles Deleuze and Felix Guattari, *Anti-Oedipus* (1999) and *A Thousand Plateaus*(1987).

sovereign subject in these pronouncements'?

For Spivak, the dismantling of the 'sovereign subject' and the realization of a counterhegemonic discourse (a truly revolutionary theory that profoundly interrogates current operations of power) must proceed through a close analysis of representational politics which demands an answer to the classic Marxian question of 'who benefits'? How does, in other words, representation both work as a signifier, and as a place from which to lobby for the represented's interests? Spivak points to Marx's discussion of representation in *The Eighteenth Brumaire of Louis Napoleon* as both an exemplary analysis of the two modes of representation and a more nuanced definition of 'class' (as will become clear in what follows, the two—representation and definition—are necessarily inextricable from each other).

Marx's definition of class is characterized by non-homogeneity; as Spivak writes, 'there is no such thing as a 'class instinct' at work here'; although of all people one would expect Marx to construct a homogenous notion of class, he instead constructs a fractured one. Spivak sees this heterogeneity of position as most useful in Marx's definition of class:

> In so far as millions of families live under economic existence that cut off their mode of life, their interest and their formation from those of the other classes and place then in inimical confrontation [*feindlich gegenuberstellen*], they form a class ...

In concert with this description, Spivak reproduces another important passage from the *Eighteenth Brumaire* that speaks to the issue of 'representation':

> The small peasant proprietors 'cannot represent themselves; they must be represented. Their representative must appear simultaneously as their master, as an authority over them, as unrestricted governmental power that protects them from the other classes and sends them rain and sunshine from above. The political influence [in the place of the class interest, since there is no unified class subject] of the small peasant proprietors therefore finds its last expression [the implication of a

chain of substitutions—*Vertretungen*—is strong here] in the executive force ... subordinating society to itself' (*CDPT* 71). [Please note that all bracketed annotations are Spivak's]

Spivak insists on the linguistic subtleties of Marx's use of the word 'represent'. She notes that in the original German, there is a significant difference between *Dartstellung*—representation as image or signifier and *Vertretungen*—representation as political 'proxy'. In Marx's initial description of the class he uses the word '*Darstellung*', yet in his discussion of their representation by a 'representative' he employs *Vertretungen*. This distinction is important because the latter carries with it an important sense of 'substitution' –of not being represented directly but through a proxy. It is this deferred representation—this representation that involves someone else speaking for the represented—that is so important to Spivak precisely because it calls into question the issue of whether those who are unable to represent their own interests—what we may now call the subaltern—can ever be represented—both for political purposes and in their modes of existence. Indeed, this is the question that both structures the essay and is its interrogative title, namely, 'can the subaltern speak'? This leads of course to another question that Spivak considers at the conclusion of the essay: if the subaltern can speak, can they also be heard?

In answering the first question—'can the subaltern speak', Spivak turns to a particular legal and political question that vexed the nineteenth-century English colonial administration in India—the issue of *sati* or the tradition/practice of widow sacrifice. Spivak locates a fruitful locus for the understanding of the possibilities of the intellectual representation of the 'subaltern' in colonial debates around *sati* and in their post-colonial critical redactions. Facetiously describing the British prohibition of sati as an instance of 'white men protecting brown women from brown men', Spivak reproduces in this (symptomatic) sentence the traditional perspective that elides and renders unrecoverable the specific experience/ agency of the 'brown women' for which the British acted as agents. The controversial space of *sati* allowed for a rearticulation of the 'colonial subject as Other':

The clearest available example of such epistemic violence [the

constitution of the 'Other' in relation to a transparent 'Self']
is the remotely orchestrated, far-flung and heterogeneous
project to constitute the colonial subject as Other. This project
is also the asymmetrical obliteration of the trace of that Other
as precarious Subjectivity … This is not to describe the 'way
things really were' or to privilege the narrative of history as
imperialism as the best version of history. It is, rather, to offer
an account of how an explanation and narrative of reality was
established as the normative one. (*CDPT* 76)

Paradoxically, even the 'subaltern studies group'—a group of
Indian intellectuals that are committed to studying the mechanisms
and effects of colonialism—is not of help to Spivak in articulating the
agency of the subaltern. Sadly, for Spivak, one of this group's premier
members—Ranajit Guha—is guilty of the same kind of homogeniza-
tion of the subaltern for which Spivak faults Deleuze and Foucault
(among others). In Guha's schematization of the various groups that
make up Indian society, the subaltern is unsatisfactorily defined as
those who are not of the 'elite': 'The object of the group's investigation, in the case not even of the people as such but of the floating
buffer zone of the regional elite—subaltern is *a deviation* from an
ideal—the people or subaltern—which is itself defined as a difference from the elite' (*CDPT* 80; italics in original). This demarcation
of the subaltern leads Spivak to ask again—'with what voice consciousness can the subaltern speak?' The methodology required to
answer this question points her to deconstruction. It is deconstruction's self-consciousness that Spivak finds most useful as a method-
ological template for the realization of a responsible representation
of the subaltern. Quoting Derrida, Spivak notes that deconstruction
'invokes an "appeal" to or "call" to the "quite-other" (*tout-autre* as
opposed to the consolidating other), of "rendering *delirious* the interior voice that is the voice of the other in us' (*CDPT* 89).

This attention to the self-reflexivity of the constitution of the
other—what Spivak calls 'the mechanics of the constitution of the
Other'—is crucially important in enabling a representation of the
subaltern female—one who is always 'doubly effaced' because of her

femaleness. In the study of *sati*, the agency of the subaltern women is almost impossible to recapture; she is effaced within legal and doctrinal defences or condemnations of the practice. The widow's psychology and motives are rendered invisible in two competing interpretations of this act; one that 'the women actually wanted to die' which is heard from nativist arguments and the other (British) that the prohibition of this practice was a means to 'save brown women from brown men'. (93) It is in between these two assertions that Spivak desires to 'plot a history', one in which we can hopefully hear the subaltern—in this case, the self-immolating widow—speak.

In order to reconstruct a history in which we can hear the voice of the self-immolating widow, Spivak turns to Hindu doctrinal discussions of *sati*. In these writing, Spivak carefully reconstructs the ideological and material context of the widow's own understanding of the social and personal significance of the ritual suicide. She locates in these doctrinal writings a curious agency associated with self-immolation; the widow who self-immolates becomes 'an extreme case of the general law' of the asymmetry of power that defined the relationship between husband and wife. Unlike the widow who declines to self-immolate, the *sati* 'will be praised by groups of *apsaras* [heavenly dancers], [and] sport with her husband as long as fourteen Indras rule' (*CDPT*, 99). As Spivak notes, *sati* was also a means of escaping from a female body that encased the woman within a somatic site of inferiority. To burn this body was to escape this status—even if this escape must proceed through death. Her reading of *sati*, then reinscribes a sense of agency or volition that traditional history rejects or effaces; it renders somewhat transparent the interests that motivated what at first seems like a simple act of patriarchal barbarism. It is important to note, however, that Spivak in no way encourages or approves of *sati*, nor, however, does she simply subscribe to the reading of it as a (transparent) case of brown men victimizing brown women.

The final section of her essay is an examination of the 1926 suicide of a young woman, Bhuvaneswari Bhaduri. A member of an armed group for Indian independence, Bhaduri committed suicide because she could not carry out an assassination to which she had been entrusted. What is noteworthy about Bhaduri's death is that she waited for the onset of menstruation before she committed suicide. In so doing, she disrupted, in Spivak's reading, a conventional interpretation that would have assumed that her suicide was a result of an illicit love affair. Her menstruation was a sign that this was not the case, and that such a reading could not be imposed upon her (dead) female body. As Spivak writes, 'Bhuvaneswari had known that her death would be diagnosed as the outcome of illegitimate passion. She had therefore waited for the onset of menstruation... . She generalized the sanctioned motive for female suicide by taking immense trouble to displace (not merely deny) in the physiological inscription of her body, its imprisonment within legitimate passion by a single male' (*CDPT* 104). As Spivak notes, her suicide, without this conventional explanation at hand, becomes absurd. It is not so much an assertion, but a confusion of motives and interests.

So, then, what are the potentialities for the subaltern to speak? Certainly, Bhuvaneswari's example succeeds in making 'delirious that interior voice that is the voice of the other in us'. Yet, Spivak ends the essay reasserting, pessimistically, that 'the subaltern cannot speak'—at least not through the conventional methods international feminism and other movements have used to make her speak. To make the subaltern speak is thus a necessarily incomplete task, but one, in being so, that is not to be avoided, but rather to be embraced. In ending, Spivak notes—in a somewhat ambiguous call to intellectual arms—that 'the female intellectual has a circumscribed task which she must not disown with a flourish' (*CDPT* 104).

Queer Theory

Queer theory expands the parameters of feminist theory by centralizing sexuality in the analysis of gender oppression. Inspired by Adrienne Rich's seminal article 'Compulsory Heterosexuality and the Lesbian Existence', discussed below, this political/theoretical movement critiqued traditional feminist critiques' marginalization of the issue of sexuality in its analysis of patriarchal culture. Queer theory is also anticipated by Monique Wittig's work, but its main concern is not only to discuss the experience of lesbians within a male-defined paradigm of gender, but to question the very foundations of our notions of sexuality and normativity—especially with regard to heterosexuality. Judith Butler, a prominent practitioner of queer theory, describes this approach as a form of 'trouble-making'; queer theory attempts to question, to disturb, to trouble identity categories (man, woman, gay, straight, lesbian, queer, transgender, and so on) and to investigate the 'political stakes' in naturalizing categories which are not at all natural, but rather the result ('effects') of certain institutional and personal power relationships. As she writes, 'the task of this inquiry [queer theory] is to centre on—and decentre—such defining institutions: phallologocentrism and compulsory heterosexuality' (Butler, *Gender Trouble*, ix). Queer theory—in its practice—is more theoretical than political, but its inquiries nevertheless lead to political activism.[1]

Having established the theoretical bias of queer theory, it is never-theless important to note its origins have a definite political base—particularly the New York Stonewall riots of 1969. These riots gave impetus toward forming a rejuvenated and radicalized gay rights agenda, and resulted in the creation of many politically-oriented

---

1 'Queer Nation' was one political group that resulted, in part, from the theoretical work in queer theory. Also, the transgender movement frequently uses queer theory in their approach to understanding sexuality and gender.

groups such as Radicalesbians (see above) as well as the New York Gay Liberation Front.[1]

Adrienne Rich

Compulsory Heterosexuality and Lesbian Existence

To a literary audience, Adrienne Rich is best known for her poetry; she has received numerous prizes in poetry—including a Guggenheim fellowship and the National Book Award in 1974. She refused the National Medal of Arts award in 1997 as a protest against President Clinton's foreign and domestic policies. Similarly, she refused to attend a White House symposium on Poetry and the American Voice in 2003 as a protest against the Iraq War.

Her poetry has a political resonance this is mirrored in essays that question the norms around femininity, masculinity and sexuality. One such essay, 'Compulsory Heterosexuality and Lesbian Existence' is regarded as a foundational text in queer theory. Written in 1980, this essay ventures into territory then unquestioned in Anglo-American feminism: the 'naturalness' of heterosexuality, the erasure of lesbian existence and the mutually defining relationship of these two phenomena. Rich's thesis is contained in the first part of the essay's title: *compulsory* heterosexuality. Arguing against those who view hetero-

---

1   Stonewall was a gay bar in New York's Greenwich Village in the 1960s and, in fact, it still exists today. At that time, the police routinely raided these bars since homosexuality was a 'criminal' act according to the state and federal statutes of the time. (In some very conservative Southern states such as Alabama, it is still considered a crime to engage in gay sex). On June 27, 1969 the police once again raided Stonewall, but this time, to their incredulity, the patrons fought back. The following newspaper account provides a sense of the rawness and explosiveness of the scene: '[T]he scene become explosive. Limp wrists were forgotten. Beer cans and bottles were heaved at the windows and a rain of coins descended on the cops ... Almost by signal the crowd erupted into cobblestone and bottle heaving' (qtd. in John D'Emilio, *Sexual Politics, Sexual Communities*, 232) There were of course other lesbian and gay rights organization predating the Stonewall riots, but this riot undoubtedly goaded the struggle into both more national visibility and more conscious acts of resistance. The first gay pride parade took place just a year later in San Francisco, and was soon followed by parades in New York and London.

sexuality as the natural bias of women and lesbianism as an unfortu-
nate deviation, Rich contends that heterosexuality is not necessarily
natural, but rather a compulsory institution for women. In fact, heterosexuality, in her view, is naturalized so that its compulsory nature
is hidden from women in order that all other behaviours are regarded
as 'unnatural'.

Rich in fact poses that the opposite may indeed be true—that instead
of heterosexuality, what is natural for women is lesbianism (although
her definition of lesbianism, as we will see, reaches far beyond the
physical). Her hypothesis is based on psychological understandings
of female children's first and most enduring bonds—towards their
mothers. As she writes,

> If women are the earliest sources of emotional caring and phys-
> ical nurture for both female and male children, it would seem
> logical, from a feminist perspective at least, to pose the fol-
> lowing questions: whether the search for love and tenderness
> in both sexes does not originally lead toward women; *why in
> fact women would ever redirect that search;* why species sur-
> vival, the means of impregnation, and emotional/erotic rela-
> tionships should ever have become so rigidly identified with
> each other; and why such violent strictures should be found
> necessary to enforce women's total emotional, erotic loy-
> alty and subservience to men. (*The Lesbian and Gay Studies
> Reader* [*TLGSR*] 232)

Rich here contends that women (and men) are profoundly bonded
to other women because of their primary relationship with their
mothers. If this is the case, then, heterosexuality must not be natural
but rather a compulsory requirement of patriarchal society. If so, then
it must be treated as one political institution among others, dependent
for its functioning upon certain strategies of exclusion, erasure, and
punishment. Since heterosexuality is a political institution, it demands
investigation and inquiry—activities that, to Rich's distress, feminist
criticism has ignored. More damagingly, feminist criticism has failed
to see heterosexuality as a compulsory political institution, but has
instead 'bought into' the fiction that heterosexuality is natural and

therefore not subject to critical interrogation. Part of Rich's essay
is a profound critique of works of feminist criticism that naturalize
heterosexuality and therefore necessarily fail to understand it as a
political construct.[1]

Once again, it is important to note that Rich does not suggest that
all women are lesbians in the traditional sense: in fact she develops
the idea of a lesbian continuum—a range of emotional and erotic
bonding in which all women can locate themselves (if allowed to do
so). The lesbian continuum is an important counter-assault to normative notions of sexuality because it renders the lesbian experience
visible, something that compulsory heterosexuality requires remain
hidden. This continuum is indeed vast, so much so that every woman
at every time and place can locate themselves upon it. As Rich writes,

> If we consider the possibility that all women—from the infant
> suckling at her mother's breast, to the grown woman expe-
> riencing orgasmic sensations while suckling her own child,
> perhaps recalling her mother's milk smell in her own, to two
> women like Virginia Woolf's Chloe and Olivia, who share a
> laboratory, to the woman dying at ninety, touched and han-
> dled by women—exist on a lesbian continuum, we can see
> ourselves as moving in and out of this continuum, whether we
> identify ourselves as lesbian or not (*TLGSR* 240).

The concept of the lesbian continuum allows us provides a new lens
for the understanding of the history of women and relocates the abuse
of women as part of socially prescribed heterosexuality. It also allows
us to review the messages of popular culture, and in particular, the
fetishization of 'romance' as part of a move towards the naturalization
of heterosexuality and the marginalization of other forms of women
bonding. Perhaps most importantly, it allows us to reconsider the
'deviance' of 'deviance'—if lesbianism—in all of its forms (sexual
and not) is part of every women's social worlds, then lesbianism as

---

1   As Rich notes about the works she considers, 'in none of them is the question
ever raised as to whether, in a different context or other things being equal,
women would choose heterosexual coupling and marriage; heterosexuality is
the presumed "sexual preference" for "most women", either implicitly or explic-
itly' (*The Gay and Lesbian Studies Reader* 229).

an accusation loses its power.

While all of the above may be the epistemological rewards of the lesbian continuum, there are nevertheless some important drawbacks. The lesbian continuum—by defining all women as in some sense 'lesbian'—eradicates the specificity of the category. What does it mean to be lesbian if all women can in some sense be lesbian? How does this identity retain its political force if it can be diluted to such an extent? While questioning the compulsoriness of heterosexuality and rendering the lesbian visible is crucial to instantiate a revolutionary 'querying' and 'queerying' of sexuality, the answer is perhaps not to make every woman a lesbian, but to naturalize lesbianism and other sexualities in the same way that heterosexuality is—and, in this way, to challenge the naturalization of any sex/gender categories.

Judith Butler

Imitation and Gender Insubordination

Judith Butler's work continues the investigations of theorists such as Adrienne Rich into the political and existential viability of categories of sexuality. Trained as a philosopher, Butler's work is heavily influenced by the works of Michel Foucault, Jacques Derrida and Jacques Lacan. She also may be seen as profound critic of categories of 'being'—of the way in which social institutions through their prohibitions and discourses create ideological 'effects' which are then naturalized as identities, norms, and so on. The beginning of one of her most important essays, 'Imitation and Gender insubordination' is an articulation of her profound discomfort with normative identity categories:

> So I am sceptical about how the 'I' is determined as it operated under the title of the lesbian sign, and I am no more comfortable with its homophobic determination than with those normative definitions offered by the members of the 'gay or lesbian community.' I'm permanently troubled by identity categories, consider them to be invariable stumbling-blocks, and understand them, even promote them, as sites of necessary

trouble. (Butler reprinted in Diana Fuss, ed. *Inside/Out* 15)

Butler is both troubled and delighted by the riskiness of identity categories. She glories in the potentialities of indeterminacy—of slippage—that any semiotic (sign) such as 'lesbian' promises and occludes. She is troubled precisely because of the various ways in which this sign is made to behave by both a homophobic community as a sign of deviance, and by the gay and lesbian movement as a sign of liberation. She asks, provocatively, 'who or what is "out" made manifest and disclosed, when and if I reveal myself as a lesbian' (15)? What Butler wants to make clear with this question is that she is not revealing a hidden essence when she 'comes out'. The traditional discourse of 'coming out' is predicated upon an 'I'—a real, true, actual self—that is released from the masks and charades of 'normative' sexuality when it steps out of the metaphorical closet. For Butler, the 'I' that comes out is just as much of a fiction as the 'I' that stayed in the closet. It is a false totalization—an attempt at ontological completeness that repudiates its own contradictions:

> If a sexuality is to be disclosed, what will be taken as the true determinant of its meaning: the phantasy structure, the act, the orifice, the gender, the anatomy? And if the practice engages a complex interplay of all of those, which one of these erotic dimensions will come to stand for the sexuality that requires them all? (17)

Butler denies any possible totalization of an 'I' or a gender/sexuality for that matter. She views identities as predicated upon what they exclude as much as what they include. In fact, sexual identities are best understood as performances; Butler, significantly, subtitles a section of this essay as 'On the Being of Gayness as Necessary Drag' (18). For Butler, ironically, 'drag'—consciously acting out a 'gender' or sexuality is the truest form of identity. It is such because in its very being it denies its own naturalness—originariness—it exults in its playfulness and in its performance. Identities that represent themselves as natural, on the other hand, are fictions. In this contention, Butler relies heavily on both Lacan and Derrida. She takes from Lacan the notion that the 'self' is a composite—constructed of exclusions, misapprehensions, fantasies, and so on.[1] She also transposes Derrida's discussion of the fictive origin of the 'logos'—the word that precedes writing—but which is actually only produced by writing— into the world of sexuality and gender. Just as the 'I' is a fractured 'I' made up of what it is not (exclusions) as much as what it is (inclusion), gender and sexuality are predicated upon exclusions, and upon a fiction of their own naturalness. Similarly, just as the concept of the logos—originary speech—depends for its existence on the writing that produces it even as it is supposed to postdate it, the normality and originariness of heterosexuality is predicated upon the 'denial' of the non-normative (gayness) that makes possible heterosexuality's presumed normativity. So, the logos and heterosexuality both claim in their assertions of originariness that there is no 'other', no exclusions, and no history of performances that grant them their authenticity as origins. But, in fact, according to Butler, gender and sexuality (heterosexuality, especially) is an effect of practices that are repeated so often they seem originary. As she writes, 'to claim that there is no performer prior to the performed, that a performance is performative, that the performance constitutes the appearance of a 'subject' as its effect is difficult to accept' (24). It is, in Butler's view, only through performance that sexuality or gender is established. We are always—consciously or unconsciously—acting out a sexuality or gender according to (or against) the norms established by society.

In this compulsion to perform, Butler locates a potential site of disruption for heterosexuality's claim to normalcy. She argues that if an identity is dependent upon repetition, then this identity is 'permanently at risk, for 'if there is … always a compulsion to repeat, repetition never fully accomplishes identity. That there is a need for repetition at all is a sign that identity is not self-identical. It requires to be instituted again and again … ' (Butler 24) And, even if the repetition is seamless, it can never hope to capture the identity completely. There is always some seepage, some extra that either threatens the

---

1   Please see Jacques Lacan's discussion of the 'mirror stage'. A full discussion of this understanding of a child's development is covered in *An Introduction to Critical Theory*, Humanities E-books 2007.

performance of a sex/gender identity or confuses its categorical dis-
tinctions from other such identities.

As a more concrete illustration of the riskiness and self-com-
promising potential of performing sexual identities, Butler looks
at butch/femme lesbian relationships. A butch/femme relationship
may be understood as one where one woman takes on a traditionally 'male' role (the butch), and the other woman the traditionally
'female' role (femme). In this dyad, Butler notices how the role of the
butch is predicated upon its inverse—that of the femme. The butch's
very identity—as a strong, dominant, husband-like partner—is completely dependent upon the femme's acquiescence to this performance. Thus, the femme has enormous power in the relationship even
though she plays the weaker sex here—dependent sexually, economi-
cally and psychologically upon her butch.

Although Butler convincingly persuades us of the performativity
of gender/sex roles, we may still wonder how such an analysis can
translate into political or social interventions. To this question, Butler
does not have a very satisfying answer. By the end of her analysis,
she seems to realize that this will be a critique of her discussion and
she attempts to anticipate it by asking herself,

> How ... to engage gender itself as an inevitable fabrication,
> to fabricate gender in terms which reveal every claim to the
> origin, the inner, the true, and the real as nothing other than
> the effects of *drag*, whose subversive possibilities ought to be
> played and replayed to make the 'sex' of gender into site of
> insistent political play? (29)

Her answer is simply to keep the play of 'drag' alive—to work both
sexuality and gender against their normative grains, and, in so doing,
to reveal their 'essential' performativity. Butler's ideal dream is for
all of us to recognize ourselves as always 'dragging'—playing a role,
a gender, a sexuality—in ways that are less patently obvious than the
traditional drag queen, but no less real.

Eve Kosofsky Sedgwick

Eve Kosofsky Sedgwick's work established the importance of applying 'queer' theory to works of literature. In her first book, *Between Men*: *English Literature and Male Homosocial Desire* she explored instances of 'homosexual panic' in nineteenth-century works by authors such as George Eliot, Charles Dickens and Alfred Lord Tennyson, among others. 'Homosexual panic' refers to the intense fear of the possibility of homosexual attachment to another man and its consequent sublimation and rerouting 'through triangular desire involving a woman' (*Epistemology of the Closet [EC]* 15). In *The Epistemology of the Closet,* Sedgwick significantly broadens her inquiry into the 'queerness' of western culture. She instantiates an 'epistemology'—a way of thinking about and understanding the dualities of homosexuality/heterosexuality and inside/out (of the closet)—that she believes is central to understanding twentieth century western culture in general. As she explains,

> I am trying to make the strongest possible introductory case for a hypothesis about the centrality of this nominally marginal, conceptually intractable set of definitional issues to the important knowledges and understandings of twentieth-century Western culture as a whole. (*EC* 2)

Sedgwick therefore is not only concerned with the effects of the homosexuality/heterosexuality duality upon literary works, but upon Western culture as a whole. In fact, she pays almost as much attention to the workings of the 'closet'—in the sense of strictures against and the silencing of homosexual identity—in both the political and social world as in literature. In part, this concern with the political ramifications of the closet is spurred by the HIV/AIDS epidemic that Sedgwick sees as contributing in both positive and negative ways to discussions about homosexuality. For many, the 'closet' is a life and death issue and ignorance (feigned or otherwise) is no longer a luxury that can be afforded.

Knowledge, after all, is not power, although it is the magnetic field of power. Ignorance and opacity collude or compete with knowledge in mobilizing the flows of every, desire, goods, meanings, persons. ... Such ignorant effects can be harnessed, licensed and regulated on a mass scale for striking enforcements—especially around sexuality, in modern Western culture, the most meaning-intensive of human activities. (*EC* 5)

As Sedgwick continues, ignorance is a potent political force, mobilizing the material oppression of victims of AIDS. 'The U.S. Justice Department ruled in June, 1986, that an employer may freely fire persons with AIDS exactly so long as the employer can claim to be ignorant of the medical fact ... that there is no known health danger in the workplace from the disease' (*EC* 5). Thus, while speaking out has always been performative—materially and socially impacting the conditions of existence of particular groups—so too has ignorance, and as is evident from the quotation above, ignorance or the pretense of ignorance is sufficient to implement prohibitive and prejudicial discourses and models of behaviour.

To combat this ignorance—or at least to take a tentative step towards such a goal—Sedgwick delineates certain 'axioms' that she feels should guide inquiry into the epistemology around sexuality and its prohibitions. While it is beyond the scope of this summary to review all of the axioms in depth, I will review a few of the key ones. The first is deceptively simple yet it expresses an important understanding of homosexuality and heterosexuality. The first axiom— 'People are different from each other'—refers not only to the most obvious differences in race, ethnicity, attitudes, age, and so on— but a less acknowledged difference—around sexuality. Sedgwick objects to the unthinking equation of certain sexualities with certain expected behaviours and sexual roles. In delineating one such difference around sexuality, Sedgwick, writes, for example, that '[e]ven identical genital acts mean very different things to different people' and also, 'for some people, sexuality provides a needed space for heightened discovery and cognitive hyper-stimulation. For others, sexuality provides a needed space of routinized habituation and cognitive hiatus' (*EC* 25).

Another axiom that is crucially important for the fruitful investigation of issues of sexuality and gender is that 'the study of sexuality is not coextensive with the study of gender; correspondingly, anti-homophobic inquiry is not coextensive with feminist inquiry. But we can't know in advance how they will be different' (*EC* 27). This is not to say that feminist inquiry does not encompass—in many cases—a study of sexuality, but that it should not be assumed that gender and sexuality are one and the same: an inquiry into gender is not necessarily an inquiry into sexuality. Sexuality—in its divergent natures— cannot always be stably 'gendered'; some acts, and some behaviors might not 'match' the gender performing them. An important aspect of anti-homophobic inquiry is to separate out these two poles and not to unthinkingly assign certain behaviors to a particular manner of performing one's sex.

Finally, at the end of this first chapter—one might say the manifesto—of *Epistemology of the Closet*, Sedgwick turns to literature. She asserts that the silencing of the always-present homosexuality possibility—the sexuality that dare not speak its name— has been a key cornerstone in Western literature and culture. Ironically, even though many of the heroes of Western philosophy and literature— Socrates, Proust, Shakespeare (among others)—contain within their works if not celebrations (Socrates) at least allusions to homosexuality (Proust and Shakespeare) they are never acknowledged openly in criticism: they are carefully kept in the critical closet. Quoting Allan Bloom[1], Sedgwick notes that the 'danger' of opening up this closet lies 'in their expression'; this expression enervates the 'reservoirs of cathectic energy that are supposed to be held ... in an excitable state of readiness to be invested in a cultural project' (*EC* 56). To expose these sublimated 'energies' is to dilute both the literary and critical project. For Sedgwick, however, it is only through the opening up of the closet—and the revelations of the underlying epistemology of secretiveness that makes possible the closet—that will lead to a more responsible critical inquiry into both gender and sexuality.

Opening the closet necessarily means the disrupting the canonicity

---

1 Allan Bloom was Sedgwick's mentor at Yale University as is the author of many books, the most famous of which is *The Closing of the American Mind.*

of the canon. Instead of complying with the restrictions and exclusions that make the 'canon' the 'canon', Sedgwick's inquiry necessarily requires 'the naming ... of a hegemonic, homoerotic/homophobic male canon of cultural mastery' (*EC 58*). It also requires, however, 'the recreation of a minority gay canon from currently non-canonical material' (*EC* 58). The canon, like the closet, must be opened up, and its assumptions, exclusions and inclusions exposed to critical analysis.

Sedgwick also demands a consciousness of the ways in which one's subject position necessarily impacts any critical project (and its reception). In order to avoid the universalizing impulse, the ethnic, class, racial and cultural biases of a critic must be as transparent as possible and considered in both external and internal (self) evaluations of the work. This attention constitutes the last axiom of the chapter, namely, 'the paths of allo-identification [other-identification] are likely to be strange and recalcitrant. So are the paths of auto-identification' (*EC* 59). Describing her own motivations for writing *The Epistemology of the Closet,* for example, Sedgwick notes the particular contents of her self-identification:

> To identify *as* must always include multiple processes of identification *with*. It also involves identification *as against*; but even did it not, the relations implicit in *identifying with* are, as psychoanalysis suggests, in themselves quite sufficiently fraught with intensities of incorporation, diminishment, inflation, threat, loss reparation and disavowal.... I can say generally that the vicarious investments most visible to me have had to do with my experiences as a woman; as a fat woman; as a non-procreative adult; as someone who is, under several different discursive regimes, a sexual pervert, and under some, a Jew. (63)

This careful delineation of identity is part and parcel of Sedgwick's goal of differentiating difference—of making the multiplicity of what is defined as difference as visible as possible and in so doing to combat the willed opacity of ignorance. For Sedgwick, ignorance is as powerful a tool of exclusion and oppression as knowledge—in fact even more so, since the ignorance is in itself unable to be questioned and therefore always already guiltless—even as it continues to fuel oppressive discursive regimes.

Wayne Koestenbaum

The Queen's Throat: Homosexuality and the Art of Singing

Wayne Koestenbaum's work may be seen within the context of Foucault-inspired history of sexuality and its attendant discourses.[1] His article, 'the Queen's Throat: Homosexuality and the Art of Singing' applies Michel Foucault's method of discourse analysis to the emergence of two different but overlapping ways of speaking and thinking about both sexuality and the voice in the 19th century.[2] In his masterful work, *The History of Sexuality*, Michel Foucault contended that a new way of thinking about homosexuality occurred in the late 19th century, coinciding with the rise of the psychological and psychoanalytic theories of sexuality. As a result of the writing of sexologists (scientists of sex and sexuality) such as Richard Von Kraft-Ebbing, Havelock Ellis and Sigmund Freud, homosexuality became an identity in the late nineteenth century. Before this time, homosexuality had not been seen as an identity, but as an act which a person should not do. Unsurprisingly, this homosexual 'discourse' was replete with prohibition, full of injunctions against acts so-called normal sexual beings should not perform, and the homosexual was defined as one who could not channel his or her sexual desires in the correct (heterosexual) direction.

Koestenbaum identifies a compelling correlation between the rise of a discourse around homosexuality (and consequently, heterosexuality) and the creation of a specific 'science' of the voice. He sees the two as distinct in some ways yet clearly intertwined in their imagery, their prohibitions, and their attitudes toward femininity and masculinity. According to Koestenbaum, the fear of a latent homosexuality

---

1   It is arguable whether or not sexuality can be separated from its discourse; certainly, Michel Foucault among others would argue that sexuality is constituted by discourse, and does not exist outside of it.

2   For a full discussion of Michel Foucault's work, see the forthcoming Humanities Insights title, *Michel Foucault.*

seeps into the science of the voice. Also, anxieties around gender and gendering similarly inflect ideologies about 'the voice':

> This ideology of 'voice' as original and identity-bestowing took root in an era that Michel Foucault has defined—a time when sexuality evolved as the darkness we year to illuminate—a constitutive hiddenness … Operatic singing doesn't represent any single sexual or gendered configuration, but it is a metaphor for how our bodies stumble into sex and gender in the first place. (206)

The voice was seen as a somatic index through which one could read a person's sexual and gender identity. The need to see the voice—the new inventions of the laryngoscope, that allowed one to peer down into the voice box—was, according to Koestenbaum, simply a symptom of a larger and much broader cultural inquiry into sexual and gender deviance. To not have the correct 'voice' or to have a voice that is not correctly gendered—such as in the case of castrati—was to disturb a natural system of sex and gender and, in so doing, to threaten the toleration of deviance. As Koestenbaum notes, the evolution of the science of the voice—what he calls 'a voice culture'—occurred with the wholesale disappearance of the castrato as a favoured voice-type.[1] The castrati were a disturbing and unacceptable presence during a period that witnessed the rise of psychoanalysis and its concomitant privileging of the phallus as key to normal male sexual identity. As Koestenbaum notes,

> both [voice culture and psychoanalysis] are hell-bent on vocalizing hidden material [the former through singing; the latter through speaking] and both take castration seriously. Voice culture desires the castrato's scandalous vocal plenitude, while psychoanalysis imagines castration to be the foundation of male and female identity. All these sexual and vocal discourses, insisting that the missing phallus means everything, zealously cast the 'castrato' as star in the epic of psychic reality. (210)

---

1   Castrati were male singers who were castrated in order to prevent the deepening of their voices.

Voice culture's task, then, in the nineteenth and twentieth-centuries, like psychoanalysis's task, was to channel this 'vocal plenitude' into acceptable expression. Since the castrato was out, it was up to the voice teachers and voice manuals to 'enforce some and not other channelings of energy through the body' (210). Unsurprisingly, the voice-box, the larynx, becomes a metaphorical sex-organ: descriptions of them are shot through/ imbued with sexual imagery. A 1948 voice manual, for example, describes the larynx as follows:

> Two thick membranes, two lips like little shutters, lying hori-
> zontally, with their opening from front to back. The opening
> between these two lips is called 'glottis'. When a vocal sound
> is produced the edges of these shutters come together firmly.
> (212)

To control this voice-box was to control sexuality. Thus, aberrations of the voice, such as the falsetto—where the male voice loses its masculinity and stumbles into a feminine range—were an embarrassment that threatened the clear divide between the natural—a correctly gendered voice and the unnatural—the homosexually-inflected voice. Although permeated by the fear of homosexuality, voice discourse was, at this time, its somatic (if not mortal) enemy. Where voice discourse strove for the correct channelling of its energies, homosexuality seemed to revel in its perversity—in the deviation of desire/energy. The control of the voice became one more cultural battleground in the implicative war against homosexuality. The brilliance of Koestenbaum's essay rests on its ability to uncover the hidden interrelatedness of two seemingly distinct discourses, and how fear and trembling about sexuality and gender spread virally throughout this as well as other cultural discourses. The continued identification of such cross-influences is vital to the historically, socially and politically resonant practice of queer theory in the 21st century.

Afterword

Who Needs Feminism?

Since the first edition of this text, grass-roots feminism has experienced a much-needed resurgence. This resurgence has been deployed through social media, such as Facebook. One prime example of this is "Who Needs Feminism". Started by a group of students at Duke University (Durham, North Carolina), "Who Needs Feminism" has grown into a worldwide phenomenon in just one year. We see evidence of the tag throughout the world today, from North Carolina, to India, to Europe and elsewhere. Women are answering this basic question differently depending upon their individual circumstances. But, the question remains imperative to ask. In a world where girls in Nigeria are kidnapped with impunity by radical Muslim terrorists, where a girl in India is brutally gang-raped while riding home on a bus (and later dies of her injuries), where 70% of all crimes "reported to police involve women" in Peru (www.un.org) where female genital mutilation is still a routine practice in many parts of Africa and Asia (affecting 85-115 million women), and where domestic violence is still the leading cause of injury for women, "Who Needs Feminism" is a wake-up call for women living in the second decade of the twenty-first century.[1] The theorists we considered in this volume never doubted that we all need

---

1   For information regarding the attack in Delhi, see Basharat Peer's article in *The New Yorker*, 2 January 2013. The attack against 'Nirbaya' (a made-up name for the anonymous woman meaning fearless) sparked protests across India especially as a result of the police chief's dismissive attitude towards the crime. After hearing of the attack, the Delhi police chief is reported to have said, "women should not go out late at night" ("After A Rape and Murder Fury in Delhi"). All information regarding the abuse of women worldwide is taken from the following sources: http://www.un.org/womenwatch/daw/vaw/, http://www.un.org/rights/dpi1772e.htm
http://www.ncadv.org/files/DomesticViolenceFactSheet%28National%29.pdf.

feminism; they knew that feminism was the only way forward for women to realize their own full humanity *and* to be treated as fully human by men. "Who Needs Feminism" reminds women today of these enduring truths and will, I hope, continue to do so for years to come.

Bibliography

Primary Sources

Abelove, H., Barale, M. and Halperin, D. (eds.) (1993). *The lesbian and gay studies reader*. New York: Routledge.

Beauvoir, S. de (1952). *The second sex*. New York: Knopf.

Butler, J. (1990). *Gender trouble*. New York: Routledge.

Collins, P. H. (1990). *Black feminist thought*. New York: Routledge.

Daly, M. (1990). *Gyn/ecology: The metaethics of radical feminism*. Boston: Beacon Press.

Deleuze, Gilles and Felix Guattari (1999). *Anti-Oedipus: Introduction to Schizoanalysis*. Trans. Eugene Holland. New York: Taylor and Francis.

Deleuze, Gilles and Felix Guattari (1987). *A Thousands Plateaus: Capitalism and Schizophrenia*. Trans. Brian Massumi. Minneapolis: University of Minessota Press.

Fuss, D. (ed.) (1991). *Inside out: Lesbian theories, gay theories*. New York: Routledge.

Irigaray, L. Trans. Catherine Porter (1985). *This sex which is not one*. New York: Cornell University Press.

Kristeva, J. (1982). *Powers of horror: An essay on abjection*. New York: Columbia University Press.

Marks, E and de Courtivron I. (eds.) (1981). *New French feminisms*. New York: Schocken books.

Moi, T. (ed.) (1986). *The Kristeva reader.* New York: Columbia University Press.

Millett, K. (1990). *Sexual politics.* New York: Simon and Schuster.

Moraga, C. and Anzaldua, G. (eds.) (1983). *This bridge called my back: Writings by radical women of colour.* New York: Kitchen Table Press

Nicholson, L. (ed.) (1997). *The second wave: A reader in feminist theory.* New York: Routledge.

Sedgwick, E. (1990). *The epistemology of the closet.* Berkeley, CA: University of California Press.

Snitow, A. Stansell, C. and Thompson, S. (eds). (1983). *Powers of desire: The politics of sexuality.* New York: Monthly Review Press.

Walker, A. (1983). *In search of our mothers' gardens.* New York: Harcourt, Brace Javanovich.

Whitford, M. (ed). (1991) *The Irigaray reader.* Cambridge, MA: Blackwell.

Williams, P. & Chrisman, L. (eds.) (1994). *Colonial discourse and postcolonial theory: A reader.* New York: Columbia University Press.

Wittig, M. (1969). *Les guérillères.* Boston: Beacon Press.

Wittig, M. (1973). *The lesbian body.* Boston: Beacon Press.

Woolf, V. (1957). *A room of one's own.* London: Harcourt, Brace.

Secondary Sources

D'Emilio, J. (1983). *Sexual politics, sexual communities: The making of a homosexual minority in the United States, 1940–1970.* Chicago: University of Chicago Press. An overview of the gay liberation movement from the 1940s to the 1970s.

Greer, G. (1971). *The female eunuch.* London: Paladin. A seminal work in feminism that wittily but closely unpacks the stereotypes, myths, sexuality of women.

Haase-Dubose, D., et al. (eds.) (2003). *French feminism: An Indian anthology.* Thousand Oaks, CA: Sage. A useful collection of essays that explores the theoretical dimensions of French feminism and its influence upon Anglo-American and Indian feminist theory.

Sellers, S. (ed.) (1994). *The Hélène Cixous reader.* New York: Routledge. A collection of essays by Hélène Cixous with illuminating commentary by the editor.

Shaktini, M. (ed.) (1985). *On Monique Wittig: Theoretical, political and literary essays.* Urbana, IL: University of Illinois Press. A collection of essays discussing the theoretical, political and literary work of Monique Wittig.

Smith, P. J. (1997). *Lesbian panic.* New York: Columbia University Press. An important work of queer theory that considers the representations of lesbianism and lesbian panic in modern British fiction.

Young-Bruehl. E. (1990). *Freud on women.* New York: Norton. A collection of Freud's writings on women, with insightful commentary by Elisabeth Young-Bruehl.

About the Author

Jennifer A. Rich is an Associate Professor in the Department of Writing Studies and Composition at Hofstra Uiversity. She offers course in the rhetoric of feminism, theories and history of rhetoric and contemporary understandings of rhetoric. She has published widely in the areas of writing studies, rhetoric, film studies, and Shakespeare, and is the author of *An Introduction to Critical Theory* in this series..

Humanities-Ebooks.co.uk

All Humanities Ebooks titles are available to Libraries through EBSCO and MyiLibrary.com

Some Academic titles

Sibylle Baumbach, *Shakespeare and the Art of Physiognomy*
John Beer, *Blake's Humanism*
John Beer, *The Achievement of E M Forster*
John Beer, *Coleridge the Visionary*
Jared Curtis, ed., *The Fenwick Notes of William Wordsworth**
Jared Curtis, ed., *The Cornell Wordsworth: A Supplement**
Steven Duncan, *Analytic Philosophy of Religion: its History since 1955**
John K Hale, *Milton as Multilingual: Selected Essays 1982–2004*
Simon Hull, ed., *The British Periodical Text, 1797–1835*
Rob Johnson, Mark Levene and Penny Roberts, eds., *History at the End of the World **
John Lennard, *Modern Dragons and other Essays on Genre Fiction**
C W R D Moseley, *Shakespeare's History Plays*
Paul McDonald, *Laughing at the Darkness: Postmodernism and American Humour **
Colin Nicholson, *Fivefathers: Interviews with late Twentieth-Century Scottish Poets*
W J B Owen, *Understanding 'The Prelude'*
Pamela Perkins, ed., *Francis Jeffrey's Highland and Continental Tours**
Keith Sagar, *D. H. Lawrence: Poet**
Reinaldo Francisco Silva, *Portuguese American Literature**
William Wordsworth, *Concerning the Convention of Cintra**
W J B Owen and J W Smyser, eds., *Wordsworth's Political Writings**
The Poems of William Wordsworth: Collected Reading Texts from the Cornell Wordsworth, 3 vols.*

* These titles are also available in print using links from
http://www.humanities-ebooks.co.uk

Humanities Insights

These are some of the Insights available at:
http://www.humanities-ebooks.co.uk/

General Titles

An Introduction to Critical Theory
Modern Feminist Theory
An Introduction to Rhetorical Terms

Genre FictionSightlines

Octavia E Butler: *Xenogenesis / Lilith's Brood*
Reginal Hill: *On Beulah's Height*
Ian McDonald: *Chaga / Evolution's Store*
Walter Mosley: *Devil in a Blue Dress*
Tamora Pierce: *The Immortals*
Tamora Pierce: *Protector of the Small*

History Insights

Oliver Cromwell
The British Empire: Pomp, Power and Postcolonialism
The Holocaust: Events, Motives, Legacy
Lenin's Revolution
Methodism and Society
The Risorgimento

Literature Insights

Austen: *Emma*
Conrad: *The Secret Agent*
T S Eliot: 'The Love Song of J Alfred Prufrock' and *The Waste Land*
English Renaissance Drama: Theatre and Theatres in Shakespeare's Time
Faulkner: *Go Down, Moses* and *Big Woods'*
Faulkner: *The Sound and the Fury*
Gaskell, *Mary Barton*
Hardy: *Tess of the Durbervilles*
Heller: *Catch-22*
Ibsen: *The Doll's House*
Hopkins: Selected Poems
Hughes: *New Selected Poems*
Larkin: *Selected Poems*
Lawrence: Selected Short Stories
Lawrence: *Sons and Lovers*
Lawrence: *Women in Love*

Morrison: *Beloved*
Scott: *The Raj Quartet*
Shakespeare: *Hamlet*
Shakespeare: *Henry IV*
Shakespeare: *King Lear*
Shakespeare: *Richard II*
Shakespeare: *Richard III*
Shakespeare: *The Merchant of Venice*
Shakespeare: *The Tempest*
Shakespeare: *Troilus and Cressida*
Shelley: *Frankenstein*
Toomer: *Cane*
Wordsworth: *Lyrical Ballads*
Fields of Agony: English Poetry and the First World War

Philosophy Insights

Agamben
American Pragmatism
Barthes
Thinking Ethically about Business
Critical Thinking
Existentialism
Formal Logic
Metaethics
Contemporary Philosophy of Religion
Philosophy of Sport
Plato
Wittgenstein
Žižek

Some Titles in Preparation

Rousseau's legacy
Dreiser: *Sister Carrie*
Fitzgerald: *The Great Gatsby*
Heaney: Selected Poems
James: *The Ambassadors*
Melville: *Moby-Dick*
Melville: Three Novellas
Shakespeare: *Romeo and Juliet*

www.ingramcontent.com/pod-product-compliance
Lightning Source LLC
Chambersburg PA
CBHW030027290326
41934CB00005B/520